P9-DUU-367

Practical Pointers to Personal PRAYER

Carrol Johnson Shewmake

REVIEW AND HERALD® PUBLISHING ASSOCIATION
HAGERSTOWN, MD 21740

Copyright © 1989 by
Review and Herald® Publishing Association
This book was
Edited by Gerald Wheeler
Cover Design by Bill Kirstein
Cover Photo by Comstock, Inc. / Michael Stuckey

Unless otherwise specified, Bible texts in this book are from the *Holy Bible, New International Version.* Copyright © 1973, 1978, International Bible Society. Used by permission of Zondervan Bible Publishers.
Bible texts credited to RSV are from the Revised Standard Version of the Bible, copyrighted 1946, 1952 © 1971, 1973.

Printed in U.S.A.

99 98 97 96 95 94   10 9 8 7 6 5 4

Library of Congress Cataloging in Publication Data

Shewmake, Carrol Johnson, 1927-
   Practical pointers for personal prayer / Carrol Johnson Shewmake.
      p.   cm.
ISBN 0-8280-0486-2

   1. Prayer.   2. Spiritual life—Seventh-day Adventist authors.   3. Sanctuary doctrine (Seventh-day Adventists)   4. Seventh-day Adventists—Doctrines.   5. Adventists—Doctrines.   I. Title.
BV215.S45 1989
248.3' .2—dc19   88-30118
                                                                 CIP

ISBN: 0-8280-0486-2

Contents

Prologue
Lord, Teach Us to Pray

L ord, teach *us* to pray!" Grown men made this request of Jesus, men who doubtless prayed daily as was the Jewish custom. Yet as they listened to Jesus' own prayers and saw the results—in His own life and in His impact upon others—they recognized their own spiritual lack.

When Jesus, worn from ministering to the multitudes, retired at night to pray and came forth refreshed the next morning, revived both in body and spirit, the disciples marveled. The people exclaimed, "Never has another man spoken as this man does! He speaks with authority. How different from the scribes and Pharisees!" The disciples suspected that the source of His exceptional power came from His prayer life. No other man *prayed* as He did.

Not only did Jesus' prayer life change Him, but the disciples themselves felt the power of His prayers for *them*. Beginning to feel sorrow for their selfishness and ignorance, they entreated Him, "Lord, teach us to pray."

We have no written record of any of the prayers of those 12 men who lived intimately with Jesus for three and a half years. Yet we know they were often with Him as He prayed. Surely they too often raised their voices aloud to God in spiritual communion. The only mention we have in the Gospels about them and their prayers is a history of disappointment and disaster. On the two occasions when they could have learned most from actual practice in prayer they failed not only Jesus but themselves.

One evening Jesus took Peter, James, and John with Him to seek solitude in which to pray. Weary after the steep climb up the mountain, the three disciples fell asleep while Jesus prayed. Suddenly a bright light and heavenly voices awakened them. In amazement they gazed upon Jesus, who now seemed almost a stranger to them. His face and clothes shone with a marvelous brightness. Two men stood speaking to Him, men who radiated the same unearthly glory. The unfamiliar voices, the brilliant light, astonished the disciples. As they watched and listened in bewilderment they heard the voice of God the Father speak from heaven, proclaiming Jesus to be the beloved Son of God. It was an awe-inspiring experience, one to cherish as long as they lived.

Yet, befuddled with sleepiness, the three men missed much of the blessing available for them. How different it would have been had the disciples been awake and totally involved in praying with Jesus that eventful night.

Yet Jesus did not give up on His disciples. Later, in Gethsemane, those same three again received the opportunity to apply the principles of prayer. Inspiration tells us that had they stayed awake and prayed with Jesus on that night, they would not have had to go through the terrible disappointment at the cross. Had they prayed with Jesus, they would have had the faith to accompany Him to Calvary (see *Testimonies,* vol. 2, p. 206). But instead sleep overtook them again.

The disciples did discover how to pray. The books written by both Peter and John and the record of Acts attest to that. Prayer seems to be best learned under crisis conditions, and the Crucifixion catapulted them into exactly that. All their eager expectations for an immediate establishment of God's kingdom, three and a half years of growing hope, shattered in one moment. The cross seemed to have destroyed everything. Their broken dreams lay in a million pieces.

Yet living with Jesus even that short time had wiped out all attraction for a sinful world from their hearts. They couldn't go back to the past, and they saw nothing ahead. Empty-hearted, they faced an empty future.

And into the void of their lives God poured the Holy Spirit on the day of Pentecost. Ever after they could pray!

1

Teach *Me* to Pray

Lord, teach *me* to pray." I too was an adult when that plea became my heart cry. Although prayer had long been a part of my daily life, yet when I encountered a crisis, I found my prayers to be weak and feeble. Wondering if God really heard them at all, I recognized my utter lack of power.

My need was terrible. I spiritually threw myself before Jesus, exclaiming, "Lord, teach me to pray or else I die!" I realized that I had to *know* that my prayers reached heaven, had to *hear* His answers. No longer could I waste time dillydallying around with polite prayers—my formal morning talk with God, my routine evening prayers, my trite little blessings on the meals. If I did not learn to know God personally in a real way, life would have no meaning for me. Prayer must be more than a pleasant flow of words to remind God of what I wanted. It must be a gasping out that I am dying of spiritual hunger and thirst, and—most important of all—a quenching of that spiritual thirst.

Because people differ greatly both in personality and in circumstances, God leads each one individually in his prayer walk. Your journey will not be just like mine. But I am telling my story because I believe that prayer is vital to salvation. Without the contact of prayer we cannot have a saving relationship with God. Surely the disciples and I were not alone in our misunderstandings about prayer. Many other Christians out there must also be groping for a living relationship with Jesus. God used many people to help me in my desperate need. His plan is that we refresh others with the spiritual drink that He has given us. Realizing that I have much yet to learn, I am not setting myself up as an authority on prayer. But I feel compelled to tell my story now.

Reared in a conservative Seventh-day Adventist home, I had come to know the Lord personally in a new-birth experience at the age of 19. At 20 I married a young minister, and together we began serving the Lord. Surely if anyone could have been counted on to know how to pray, it should have been I!

But a totally unexpected crisis made it seem that my life would never be happy again. And I could do nothing tangible about it. It was then that I discovered I wasn't even sure that God heard my prayers—at least not all of them, anyway.

It wasn't as though I knew nothing about prayer. I had always enjoyed praying. Both public and private prayer had always been easy for me. Over the years I had even collected an interesting assortment of answers to my prayers. But suddenly I realized that God and I had to be more than pleasant acquaintances on good terms with each other. We must have an intimate family relationship.

Searching for answers to my many questions about prayer, I read book after book on the topic, absorbing forms and methods of prayer, reasons for prayer, stories of answers to prayer. I needed to know what prayer *did*. Was it only busy work, assigned by an exacting God? If prayer changed only *me* and not those I prayed about, then why pray for others? Much better to spend the time praying for myself. Since the crisis in my life involved my children, I needed to know that my prayers for them really made a difference. Was God really interested in my life and that of my family? Could He, *would* He, actually intervene in our lives? I kept reading.

One little book, *The ABC's of Prayer*, by Glenn Coon, aroused a spark of hope in my heart. I had read so many lovely, encouraging statements about prayer from so many people that I almost felt about to drown in the pool of wisdom. But here I found *practical* advice for daily prayer. Glenn Coon made sincere asking of God in faith (*expecting* answers) sound easy. He stated that I can take any promise in the Bible that God has made to anyone and, if I am in a similar situation, I can ask (Matt. 7:7), believe (Mark 11:24), and claim, and give thanks that I have received it (John 11:41). Naturally I determined to try this kind of prayer.

I had always been faithful at morning devotions. When my children were still babies, I began awakening in the early-morning hours to study and pray. However, I had always received much more satisfaction from my reading than from my prayers. And that seemed just as it should be to me. After all, when I read the Bible or spiritual books, wasn't God speaking to me? During my prayers, wasn't I speaking to God? Wasn't it right that God's speaking should take up the most time and be the most important?

The immediate problems I needed to overcome in prayer were many. Having always had a tendency to go to sleep whenever it is dark or whenever I close my eyes, I often dozed off on my knees. Handy sometimes, but annoying during prayer. Constantly my busy mind would begin the day's work ahead of me. Or my thoughts would just take off on someone or something for which I was praying, and soon they would be miles away. Sometimes my prayers seemed nothing more than daydreaming—and a little burdensome.

Finally I decided to make my new prayer time as different as possible from my past routine devotions. Not wanting to give myself a chance to fall asleep while praying, I set the stage carefully for my first experiment in ABC praying. Pulling up an easy chair close to the sofa in my husband's study, I arranged the lighting to a comfortable brightness, took my Bible in my hand, and invited God to sit in the easy chair as I sat on the sofa. Please understand that I was not being purposefully innovative. I was desperate for a relationship with God that I could count on, something *real.* I needed to know God in as tangible a way as I did my husband and children.

Previously I had delighted in praying in my thoughts. It was so quick, so smooth, but also so easy to drift off into daydreaming. So this morning I spoke aloud to God as to a personal friend.

"Dear Father," I said out loud, "please take that easy chair. I have such a lot I need to talk to You about this morning." It tumbled out, my urgent needs, my children, my weaknesses. Opening my Bible, I reminded God of His promises. Of how much I needed His forgiveness, His wisdom. As I read specific verses, I found comfort in the words of God.

The time passed quickly, and soon I discovered it was time to begin my day's work. That day bloomed with hope and joy, and I could hardly wait until the next morning and my talk with God. And so it went. Each morning I would wake up with a sense of expectancy, a feeling familiar to me as a child but long gone from the adult me. I liked it!

Prayer time became the focal point of my entire day. I explored the Bible, talking to God as I read. Finding promises written down in God's Word that fit my need and then claiming them for myself doubled my faith in one giant leap. Lack of faith is, I believe, the greatest impediment to the average Christian's prayer life. If you have not prayed specifically for something, you cannot even recognize the answers to your prayers when you receive them. When you pray for a specific need or purpose that you realize that God wants to give you, you just *know* He will answer. Using God's Word for the basis of my praying was the biggest factor in bringing meaning to my prayer life.

Then I discovered something else I had been doing unconsciously. When the clock told me it was time to go to the kitchen to start lunches and breakfast, it was with a feeling of sorrow that I left the study. It was as though I escorted God to the front door, saying, "Father, it's been so good to talk to You this morning, but my time is up and I'll have to say goodbye, much as I'd like to visit longer. I have to go to work. Goodbye, Father." And I would close the door on Him.

With mounting excitement I recognized that it did not have to be that way. Now I invited God to go with me from the study to the kitchen, and talk with me as I worked. Obtaining a notebook that I could stand upon my kitchen counter, I wrote a list of people to pray for, a different list for each day of the week. Then as I worked around the house and passed through the kitchen I would pause and pray for one person or family until I had finished the list for that day. Also I tried to remember that whenever the doorbell or the telephone rang, God had sent the person on the other end to me as a personal trust.

Exciting things began to happen in my life. Not only did I learn to love Bible reading, but I began to like housework! Always before, I had considered the latter merely a necessary evil, but now I discovered that I could learn spiritual lessons from it as well as from Bible reading. As I ironed I thanked God for removing the wrinkles in my life and making it smooth and beautiful. Washing dishes recalled to my mind that Christ's blood removes sin and makes me as clean and shiny as a china plate. When I scrubbed the windows I rejoiced that the Sun of righteousness shines in through the clean windows of my soul.

As I write these words I realize it sounds as though I *deliberately* thought of such things as I worked. Not so! They came spontaneously and became the joy of my days. God planted them in my eager heart to draw me continually to Him. Every day was special, and the presence of God was near me.

Summary

Since prayer is the only means of sustaining a *living* relationship with God, it is of supreme importance to the Christian that he have a living prayer life.

Things that have personally helped me in my prayer life:

1. Making specific requests based upon specific Bible promises.

    a. Ask (Matt. 7:7).

    b. Believe (Mark 11:24).

    c. Claim and give thanks (John 11:41).

2. Speaking aloud in prayer.

3. Being honest with God about my angers, fears, hostility, and needs.

4. Not only setting aside an early-morning time with God, but consciously remembering Him in prayer throughout the day.

2

Experimental Prayer

Do you recall my questions about prayer? Was it something to change only me, or would it actually transform others for whom I prayed? That is, Was it really worthwhile to pray for others? If so, why? What happens to others when I pray for them?

As I began to know God in a new and living way through my prayer time, it was obvious that the initial transformation was surely in me. In spite of my problems, life was joyous again. My faith in the Lord grew quickly. But as He changed me it was plain that others around me changed too. A long-absent peace and joy filled our home and spilled over to all I encountered.

Yet I remembered biblical counsel to pray even for government officials whom I would never have the chance to meet. Why would God ask me to pray for those I would never reach with the influence of my personal presence? Was it possible that my prayers could alter them, also? If not, then why pray?

As I questioned the Lord, I remembered the many times the Scriptures tell us to spiritually intercede for others. I could not believe that God ever assigns prayer as busy work.

"How does it work, God?" I asked.

The understanding I came to was this: Every human being has a responsibility for the part he must play in earth's history. In every individual God has put a channel of influence that He uses to reach out to the world. He has given each of us the opportunity to touch the lives of others through prayer, even though we may never meet them personally. Our prayers make it possible for God to do for them what He could not do if we did not pray.

Satan claims the world as his because of sin. Since part of God's inherent character is freedom, He will never use force in commanding obedience from His creatures. He leaves men free to choose whom they will serve—God or Satan. Thus the Lord cannot arbitrarily step into any person's life. He would be violating the law of freedom if He did so. Always quick with a comeback, Satan would immediately charge Him with unfairness. Yet Satan also knows that in the beginning, before the entrance of sin, God had created human hearts with the desire and ability to share with others what they themselves had received from God. Sin alone made man totally self-serving. The new-birth experience re-creates this original desire and ability in man. Satan knows that he cannot charge Jesus with taking unfair advantage when He answers our prayers for others, since it was part of the Creator's original plan. The devil understands more than most Christians do the power of intercessory prayer. Our prayers totally silence his accusations and give God the opportunity to work in behalf of many who might never have sought Him without our prayers. The prayers of Christians form an atmosphere of hope around the world.

Of course, it's obvious that we cannot each pray individually for every other human being living on our planet. That would make prayer a burden too heavy to bear, but God, in His great love, will direct us by the Holy Spirit to the specific persons for whom we should pray. And when the Spirit leads us to pray, we will discover that we can do so with great power.

Many Christians believe that it is inevitable that the first love for God will cool and enthusiasm fade. It doesn't have to be that way. Just as in a marriage love changes with time, so it will in a marriage relationship with God. But enthusiasm can last. The love grows deeper, the understanding greater, the responsibilities become plainer. Discouragement will come and darkness will sometimes hide the face of God for a moment, but faith will pierce the gloom and hope will glow even in spiritual night. The only time we can lose the Lord is when we turn away from Him. And even if we do that, He is ever willing and excited about taking us back. Let's not forget that!

Another important element of a successful prayer life is regularity, a consistent early-morning time with God. For me it helps to have a special spot where I pray every morning, a spot uncluttered with work reminders. In the beginning I used my husband's study. Now, in another house, and many years later, the living room is my morning chapel. (I grow to love the place I share so much with Jesus. As I pass through my living room throughout the day I often find myself recalling the experiences of the morning.

Never leave the element of reverence and awe out of prayer. Although I did not kneel in the beginning as I began my ABC praying, before many weeks I found myself once more upon my knees with closed eyes in *awe* at the wonder of conversing with the Ruler of the universe. But the prayer of a humble supplicant reaches the throne of God, whatever his posture. True prayer has great freedom.

My radical departure from my usual mode of praying was important in the beginning to jar me out of my prayer rut. Also, the change from the "thees" and "thous" of the beautiful prayer language I so loved, to everyday English, was necessary for me so that I could feel free to converse with God anytime and anywhere. Speaking aloud in prayer is still an important part of my morning devotions, protecting me from daydreaming and drifting thoughts. Although prayer has a distinct *form,* just as does a letter or conversation, yet we can widely vary that form. Sometimes I sing either at the beginning or ending of my prayer, and sometimes even shout praises. It depends, of course, on how inhibited you are or how private you can be. Surely you don't want to embarrass or annoy anyone. In some circumstances, I find that I can only whisper. We all differ in personality and custom. God wants our praise and our prayers in our own individual manner. Seek to know God in your own way, realizing that the possibility of *excitement* as well as peace lies in your prayer life.

Before I go any further, let me make a few explanations. Should I say "God told me" or "God said to me," I am not claiming any special revelation from God not available to all. I do not have visions or dreams, neither do I hear an audible voice. What I do sense is the inner voice of the Holy Spirit speaking to me through impressions. Of course, it's true that not all such impressions are reliable. However, I have discovered that as I speak more often and more intimately with God, I can learn to distinguish His voice from the other ones in my mind. Let me give you an example of how God speaks to me:

One Friday morning as I was praying, the words of Revelation 3:20 came to my mind. Here Jesus says, "Behold, I stand at the door, and knock: if any man hear my voice, and open the door, I will come in to him, and will sup with him, and he with me" (KJV). As I rejoiced that Jesus really does come in, the voice continued. "You know how busy you are when preparing for company for Sabbath dinner? How you have such a time choosing a menu? Well, when I come in to eat with you, you don't have to give the food a thought, for I will bring the supper." By that I understood that I could freely invite Jesus into my heart, for He abundantly supplies spiritual food.

I got up from my prayer time and immediately went into my hectic Friday routine. As the day progressed, I got busier and busier. After all, I was expecting a dozen people for dinner after church.

That evening at our Friday night Bible study sharing time, many related how God had blessed them during the week. I felt a nudge from God. "Tell them," He said, "what I told you this morning." Of course I related it to the group, and they rejoiced with me.

When God sends us a personal blessing, He usually plans that we share it with others. But occasionally the Lord gives us something entirely for us alone. Talking about those moments with Him would be like telling your inmost secrets aloud. Ask the Lord what He wants you to share. He will encourage you to tell about some blessings and keep quiet about the times He meant for you alone. Sometimes it may be appropriate to relate even an intimate blessing in a general way for the benefit of others. Let the Lord guide you. A blessing shared with others often becomes more real to you. It is then indelibly imprinted in your memory to look at again and again. If possible, *write* it down. Often as I reread stories from my spiritual notebook I am especially blessed again.

After He told me about His bringing spiritual food, Revelation 3:20 became special to me. I felt that God, in His great mercy, had opened up for me its inner meaning and that now I understood that text more deeply. In a special way it had become mine.

Then yesterday morning as I thanked the Lord for the spiritual food He provides so liberally for me, He repeated the verse to me again, this time with emphasis on the part that says, "*I* will come in and *eat* with him." Before, I had concentrated on what He was bringing *me* to eat. Now He was talking about *Himself* eating. Bewildered, I asked, "What do You mean, Lord, that *You* will eat? You don't need to eat. You are the embodiment of food." I tried to remember any place in Scripture where it speaks of *God* eating. Later that morning as I ironed I remembered that after Jesus' resurrection He appeared to the 11 in the upper room and they reacted with fright, believing Him to be a ghost.

"Bring me something to eat," Jesus requested, and He ate in their presence to show how real He was, how truly alive.

What God was telling me, again through Revelation 3:20, was that when He knocks at my heart door and I open it to Him, He not only brings the supper for *me* to partake of, but He *Himself* also eats with me to show how *real* His relationship with me is. (Incidentally, the experience also emphasized to me again that I will never plumb the depths of any Bible passage. Although the verse becomes especially mine after spiritual revelation, yet there is always much, much more to learn.)

I hope my little experience will illustrate what I mean when I say, "God told me." God speaks to me exactly the way Jesus promised His disciples He would to them after He returned to heaven—through the voice of the Comforter. "My sheep listen to my voice," Jesus said. "I know them, and they follow me" (John 10:27).

I believe that God wants to sharpen our hearing and seeing. I fear that often when He speaks to us, we do not know it is His voice, or if we recognize it, it almost immediately gets drowned out in the cares or pleasures of life.

Learning to pray is learning to hear the voice of God clearly.

Summary

Because God has put a channel of influence in every individual, we have the opportunity to touch the lives of others through intercessory prayer. Our prayers make it possible for God to do for them what He could not do if we did not pray.

Things I personally find helpful in making my prayer time real:

1. Regularity—consistent, early-morning time with God.

2. A special place to pray, uncluttered with everyday work.

3. Freedom to speak aloud in ordinary language—no "thees" and "thous."

4. Expectation that God will speak to me through His Word and mental impressions.

CHAPTER

3

Prayer
in Crisis

Sometimes life's burdens pile up, one after the other, until it seems impossible to dislodge them. It was like that for me. I have always found it hard to keep my mind on prayer in the midst of distractions such as a vacation, a move, or overnight guests. Until I can go back to my usual satisfying morning sessions with God, I decide a quickie prayer will have to do. As for studying—my mind is much too distracted for that. Then my entire life becomes a distraction.

One such incident began with a routine move. My husband changed pastorates after 11 years in one church. Instead of looking for a job in the new location, I decided I would first finish the college degree I had been working on for several years. Then I would take time to do the things I had always wanted to do but could never find opportunity for. I would write, give Bible studies, cultivate hobbies. Our last child was leaving home as we moved; the rest were already grown up and married. Now was the chance for me to start a new life.

We made the decision to build the house of our

dreams near our new church. All our married life we have enjoyed entertaining our church members in our home —suppers, Sabbath dinners, afternoon sings, evening Bible studies. We have found that small groups meeting in the intimacy of a home cultivates closeness in a way that church buildings cannot. So we planned a house this time with a fabulous kitchen big enough for cooking classes, and a living room large enough for a grand piano, an organ, and a host of people. Designing and decorating our new home, along with going to college, would be my first priority.

Our dream never became reality. Because my husband had been in charge of erecting several churches and we had built our own home once before, he felt confident of his ability to oversee the construction of our house. And he was capable. But prices of supplies rose, and we had to make structural changes. It became obvious that we had gotten involved in a costly mistake. Meanwhile our belongings remained packed while we lived in a little rental house, then in our daughter's home for two months, and finally in the unfinished attic room over the garage in our new house. It became more and more apparent to us that we must finish and sell the house and begin again.

When you're cooking or sewing and something turns out wrong, you can just throw out the bad batch and start all over. You can't do that with life. Some things become so muddled that only gradually can we straighten them out, and even then life *never* goes back to where it was before the mistake. Money lost is gone. Life must be lived a different way.

"O Lord, where are You? What are Your plans for us? Are You going to let us lose everything—our house, our money, and perhaps even our reputations—to teach us a lesson?" I knelt by the bed in an unfamiliar room, agony welling up into my throat, my stomach in a knot, my heart torn and wrenched with weeks of worry and discouragement. What had happened to my relationship with God? Where were all our beautiful dreams? Nothing seemed steady in my life anymore. How could my husband continue pastoring a church with this personal worry hanging over him? How had we gotten into this, anyway? Had we dishonored God's name with our poor judgment? What was going to happen next?

"God, God," I cried in desperation, "what are Your plans for us?"

"I know the plans I have for you." Clearly, amid the confusion in my heart, I heard those eight words. The panic of the past few months had almost succeeded in blocking out the voice of God. Yet I knew He was speaking to me. Still on my knees, I reached for my Bible, certain that the words I had just heard were part of a Scripture verse. Eagerly I searched, finding it in Jeremiah 29:11: " 'For I know the plans I have for you,' declares the Lord, 'plans to prosper you and not to harm you, plans to give you hope and a future.' "

Relief, joy, and gratitude flooded my heart. "You're still there, God," I breathed, "and You're not going to desert us now. Oh, thank You, thank You!"

With hope reborn I was able once more to meet each day with expectancy. Not that our problems were solved immediately—they were not. To be truthful, they are still in the process of being worked out at this writing. What did happen was that I could now believe that God had a way of escape for us. And in finding that way I discovered new depths in my relationship with Jesus.

It has been hard for me to understand how God could have let us fall into such a far-reaching error in judgment when we felt we were sincerely seeking His will. Two inspired statements have helped me.

> Do you make mistakes? Do not let this discourage you. The Lord may permit you to make small mistakes in order to save you from making larger mistakes. Go to Jesus, and ask Him to forgive you, and then believe that He does (*In Heavenly Places,* p. 124)

> If he [in this case—me!] seeks the Lord with humility and trust, every trial will work for his good. He may sometimes seem to fail, but his supposed failure to reach the place where he hoped to stand may be God's way of bringing his advancement. He thinks that he has failed, but his supposed failure means a better knowledge of himself and a firmer trust in God. . . . He may make mistakes, but he learns not to repeat these mistakes. United with Christ, the True Vine, he is enabled to bear fruit to the glory of God . . . (*ibid.,* p. 28).

About a year before this traumatic experience a small women's prayer group to which I belonged chose Jeremiah 33:3 as their theme. "Call to me and I will answer you and tell you great and unsearchable things you do not know." How apt that verse seemed for me! In my walk with Jesus I had just begun to recognize how little I really comprehended the things of God. I was encountering so many "unsearchable things" in my studies and meditation. The human nature of Christ baffled me. Even the elite minds of Adventist theological circles couldn't agree on it. How could anyone expect me to understand? Righteousness by faith—just what did the term *Righteousness by faith* really encompass? What actually happened to a person when he was born again? Why couldn't I stop sinning? And how did the Seventh-day Adventist understanding of the heavenly sanctuary relate to me personally? Was the teaching merely theory? Did it all happen in heaven or did it have an immediate impact upon me here on earth?

About this time I listened to a set of tapes by Dick Winn entitled *Adventism's Distinctive Mission*. Winn states that God has only four avenues of dealing with mankind and He never varies from them: Truth, Time, Freedom, and Love. I have never forgotten that list because it was so simple, yet made such beautiful sense. It showed such a contrast between my dealings with others and the way God dealt with me.

I recount these two incidents here because I have since realized how closely they relate to what was happening to me. Never is a sincere, honest prayer uttered but that God answers it. In all of the traumatic experiences of my life God sought to reveal to me those "great and unsearchable things" I did not know. What I did not then realize was that preconceived ideas, attitudes, prejudices, and even cherished sins blocked my understanding of the deep things of God. He, in His great love, was digging down in my heart to bring the obstructions to the surface. But always He left me *free*. He gave me *time* to choose Him in every area of life. Only *truth* could further His purposes. And His *love* never gave up on me.

Looking back on the whole experience of building our house, we can see many things we would do differently if we had it to do over again. Hindsight is always so much better than foresight. But even then we knew God was able and willing to direct His children in temporal as well as spiritual matters. Thus, it was our great desire to be so in tune with Him that we could discern His voice in our daily affairs.

Added to our house and financial perplexities, the growing problems of one of our adult children created a strained interfamily relationship. The mushrooming load of burdens seemed to me to be more than I could bear. It often left me near panic. My prayers circled around one word: *help!*

Not only did my husband and I struggle with our personal problems, but our congregation found itself in the midst of a theology and power struggle that threatened to destroy it. It seemed to my husband that his entire life's work was evaporating before his eyes. Ministerial burnout haunted his days and troubled his nights.

Our only comfort was remembering the promise God had given us through Jeremiah 29:11. " 'For I know the plans I have for you,' declares the Lord, 'plans to prosper you and not to harm you, plans to give you hope and a future.' " We hung on, longing to see the hand of the Lord reach out and solve our problems. The psalms of David were my favorite reading.

> Satisfy us in the morning with your unfailing love,
>> that we may sing for joy and be glad all our days.
> Make us glad for as many days as you have afflicted us,
>> for as many years as we have seen trouble (Psalm 90:
>> 14, 15).
> Weeping may remain for a night,
>> but rejoicing comes in the morning (Psalm 30:5).

Oh, how I longed for the morning!

About this time my husband scheduled an evangelist to present to our congregation a seminar on how to give Bible studies. Gary Ford had written an excellent book on the subject, entitled *The ABCs of Bible Study.* To my husband's delight he learned that he himself had been the minister who had baptized Gary when the young man was just 17. As John saw the ministry that Gary was doing, it lifted his own spirits. Surely God was allowing the impact of his lifework to continue.

As Gary spoke to us about how to give Bible studies he talked a great deal about prayer, relating his personal experiences with prayer during his college days and as he began his ministry. He told us how important he felt it was to him to set aside *hours* on his knees in communion with God. His comment startled me. While I usually spent at least an hour each morning in my devotions, the major part of it consisted of reading and study. An hour on my knees praying? What would I say?

Gary even suggested timing ourselves by the clock to get us started in praying longer. If he had been a different sort of person than he appeared to be, I would have just dismissed his ideas as a severe case of fanaticism. But Gary was obviously not a fanatic. Loving nothing more than to teach the Word of God, he made every conversation Christ-centered.

So I began experimenting with timed prayers. It was a fierce struggle to keep my mind on praying for more than 15 minutes. Whenever I thought about my personal problems, panic threatened to take over. But it is hard to say "Help, help" for an entire hour. So I talked about my weaknesses and failures and about God's great power and His promises. I even began again to tell Him about the "great and unsearchable things" that I did not know. "Lord, teach me to pray" was still my intense prayer.

Learning to listen for the voice of God amid deep personal anxiety is perhaps the hardest lesson in the heavenward walk. At least it has been for me. It was so much easier for me to read than to pray and meditate. I just could not keep my mind on prayer for any long period of time when disaster seemed perpetually about to fall upon me. Occasionally I would have a day when the presence of God seemed strong, but more often I barely hung on. Finally I decided that lengthy praying was right for Gary, and for Jesus, but it just didn't work for me. Slipping back into my more comfortable short prayer and longer study time, I longed for the day when God would begin to prosper me as He had promised. (What I didn't realize at that time was that as soon as I claimed the promise God began to fulfill it. Fear cast a shadow over my life that nearly hid the bright face of hope. But God showed me that later.)

In one of Gary's afternoon seminars he mentioned another young minister, Larry Ammon, a member of the Personal Ministries Department of our conference, who had had great success with his Bible studies. "Why don't you talk to him?" Gary suggested to my husband. "He might be able to help you decide upon a plan to get your church to working."

That same week John received a memo from the conference Personal Ministries Department urging any pastor interested in church renewal to contact Larry. My husband decided that it was no coincidence that circumstances brought Ammon to his attention twice in one week. He immediately telephoned him at the conference office. The conference official suggested that he and John get together at our church two mornings each week and study the Gospel of John together.

I think Ammon must have recognized the desperation, the longing in John's voice, even over the phone. At his first meeting with my husband he said, "I'd like to become a part of your life. I plan to stay around awhile." He also suggested that John invite any of his church leaders who were available those two mornings to join the studies. So

John asked the pastor's wife—me! We began a small group, six of us, that continued for the next year and a half.

God's wonderful plan was unfolding—for us individually, and for our congregation.

Summary

Listening for the voice of God amid deep personal anxiety is perhaps the hardest lesson to learn in the heavenward walk.

Things that have helped me in such times:

1. Remembering specific promises God has given me in the past, such as Jeremiah 29:11: " 'For I know the plans I have for you,' declares the Lord, 'plans to prosper you and not to harm you, plans to give you hope and a future' " (NIV).

2. Going actively forward in Christian service. Starting a prayer group. Choosing to spend time with others who are seeking the Lord. Praising God often.

CHAPTER

4

Prayer Is a Conversation

Praying with others is a stimulating change from the wholly self-centeredness of doing so alone. You sense the needs of others, you look into their hearts and share their longings, you hear prayers put into words that you yourself would never use. It leaves you marveling at the diversity of expression, of gifts. The experience adds a dimension completely new.

We met two mornings a week, Monday and Wednesday, and read a chapter from the book of John. Larry encouraged us to apply the story personally, to put ourselves into the incidents, and to be honest: Who am I in the story? The sinner. Who was Jesus? God. Conviction, confession, and commitment became our heart cry.

From the very first, Larry stressed learning to listen to the voice of God. He pointed out that only in responding to the voice of Jesus were people healed, changed, cleansed, throughout the chapters of John. And God is still the same. It is only by listening to and following the voice of Jesus that lives can be transformed today. A permanent difference in us or those we are working for can result only through the Word of God.

We didn't become a closed group, either. From the first morning Larry encouraged us to begin studying the book of John with someone else. Find someone with a need, he would emphasize, and seek to fill it. So each one of us began to meet with someone else.

The second morning we read the second chapter of John. The two stories in that chapter, applied personally, humbled each of us. We were still new at this and didn't know each other all that well. But as we prayed around the circle our supplications were for forgiveness and cleansing. Broken voices replaced self-confidence. Then Larry surprised us. As we completed the circle, Larry announced, "Let's pray around again," and he began. I almost panicked, having said it all the first time around. What more could I say? Yet I found when it came my turn, I did have more to say. The first time around had been only surface. Now God reached into the depths of my heart and brought out desires and longings I did not know I had in me. The power of the Spirit was evident in our little room. Tears of repentance and rejoicing blended together.

As the weeks progressed, we learned much about prayer. One morning Larry asked us about our private prayer life. "What is the ratio of the time you spend each day in prayer to the time you study?" he asked.

No one replied quickly so since I am often, like Peter, ready to speak, I answered. "I spend about one third as long praying as I do reading, I would imagine. Sometimes even more time than that in study."

He smiled. "Try turning the ratio around."

Instantly I felt defensive. "When I pray I am talking to God. When I read the Word He is talking to me. It's only right that He do more of the talking."

The look Larry gave me then was almost sad. "Well, I guess if you think of prayer like that, you might be right."

Pondering his expression and reply for a long time, I wondered, "What other way *is* there to look at prayer? Isn't it *me* talking to God?" Then I began remembering the way God had led me in the past in my prayer time. Had not He shown me that prayer is a *conversation* with Him—not just me talking to Him, but Him speaking to me also? A *relationship* that grows each day?

I seem to be a slower learner in spiritual things. Although I catch sight of something important from one angle, when the picture or perspective changes, I forget the very truth I have already glimpsed! Habits and concepts of a lifetime continue cropping up long after I think I have discarded them. Then, too, fear sometimes looms so large that it blocks my spiritual sight.

Larry was not suggesting that I spent too much time in Bible reading or even that I cut back on it. Rather, what he was saying was that without more prayer I couldn't even understand what I was reading. Remembering Gary's hours in prayer, I began rising half an hour earlier than usual.

It was great. I talked to God about the concepts we were learning from the book of John, spoke to Him about the things I saw that needed to be changed in my life. God, in turn, brought to me insights about commitment and dedication, love and service.

Sometimes. The above paragraph describes my devotional life *some* of the time. Other days I had no sense of the presence of God at all. Yet my faith in Him never wavered. I always knew He was there—just why He did not choose to reveal Himself to me I did not know. But I remembered that Ellen White said we are not to go by feeling but by faith.

One morning I mentioned these times to Larry.

"My faith in God is strong," I told him. "I know God is with me, even though I cannot feel His presence."

"You're right that God is always with you, even when you cannot sense His presence," he answered. "But you know," he continued, "you don't have to put up with dark times in prayer. You can pray *through* them. You can have a warm, fruitful prayer experience *every day*."

Really? I stared at him in amazement, having never heard such a thing in my entire life. Sometimes I would go weeks at a time, basking in the open presence of God. Then I would come to a dark, dry period that would, perhaps, last just as long. It was something that I accepted as a natural part of life. As far as I knew, all Christians struggled with such times. What about panic? And fear? And dreariness?

"How?" The question burst forth from me. "How do you pray through them?"

Larry wasn't much for just talking—and he never offered advice. Anything he said you could be sure came from his own personal experience.

"Try asking the Lord to reveal to you what it is that is casting a shadow across your path," he suggested. "Bare your soul before the Lord and tell Him how much you desire to be wholly His. Be in earnest."

So I began telling God about my great longing to be completely His in every part of my life. I reaffirmed my commitment to Him often during the day by breathing the prayer "Lord, I'm Yours. I desire nothing except to be wholly Yours." Many of the prayers of David in the Psalms that had often touched a responsive chord in me were of this type.

> O God, you are my God,
>   earnestly I seek you;
> my soul thirsts for you,
>   my body longs for you,
> in a dry and weary land
>   where there is no water (Psalm 63:1).

> As the deer pants for streams of
>   water,
> so my soul pants for you,
>   O God.
> My soul thirsts for God, for the
>   living God.
> When can I go and meet with God? (Psalm 42:1, 2).

> The Lord is my light and my
>   salvation—
>   whom shall I fear?
> The Lord is the stronghold of my
>   life—
>   of whom shall I be afraid? (Psalm 27:1).

> My heart says of you, "Seek his face!"
>   Your face, Lord, I will seek (verse 8).

> Whom have I in heaven but you?
>   And earth has nothing I desire
>   besides you.
> My flesh and my heart may fail,
>   but God is the strength of my heart
>   and my portion forever (Psalm 73:25, 26).

I began to find that whereas in the past I had counted on *time* to chase away the darkness of fear or routine, now I could see the power of God in prayer freeing me *immediately*. The key to such freedom was in purposefully and wholeheartedly reaching out to God. It excited me. Here was a new breakthrough in my prayer life.

Isn't it wonderful how the Lord works in our individual lives to lead us to just the people who can help us see our mental and spiritual blocks to growth? It is the Lord's will that each of us touch other lives for Him. We are to comfort and help others with what God has given us. Although my husband and I were older in years and Christian experience than both Gary and Larry, yet God used them to shake us loose from the time-worn ruts of our thinking. They led us to think new thoughts and try new prayers.

Over the years it has been hard for me to learn to accept help from a person in a face-to-face encounter. Never a "camp follower" type of person, I doubt that I would have been one of the women who traveled with Jesus. Most likely I would have openly accepted Jesus only after His death and resurrection. I need time and space to evaluate, to personalize. More often *books* have touched and changed me. They give me the necessary climate for thinking and evaluating. Yet God is slowly leading me into relationships with other Christians from whom I learn important truths.

Summary

It is only by listening to and following the voice of Jesus that lives can be changed. Permanent transformation in our own lives or in the lives of those we are working for can result only from direct application of the Word of God.

Things that have personally altered not only my prayer life but my entire outlook are:

1. Breaking the routine of prayer by praying around the circle the second or third time in our small prayer group.

2. Realizing—and putting into practice—the reality of prayer as a conversation with God.

3. Learning to reach out purposefully to God, crying, "Lord, I'm Yours. I desire nothing except to be wholly Yours."

4. Listening to and trusting other Christians as God's representatives.

CHAPTER
5

The Framework
of Prayer

I'm an orderly person. Years as a school librarian have taught me the value of a *system* in organizing things. Any possibility of understanding the Bible as a whole often seemed hopeless to me because it seemed so *unorganized*. Then God showed me a connecting thread throughout Scripture that made the stories of the Bible one long continued narrative of His intervention in the lives of humanity. This thread of unity is a relationship between God and man called the everlasting covenant.

It relieved me to discover that God always deals with His children in a systematic way. I spent days and weeks exploring the theme of the covenant. As I found that His standard for salvation was just the same in the Old Testament, the New Testament, and today, I gained new confidence. God would take care of the whole sin episode. After all, every story has to have an ending. His rescue mission to this one small erring planet is no exception. God has told us that the total eradication of the enemy is inevitable. That was good news!

The aspect of the everlasting covenant that brought the

most joy to me was that I was important in God's sight and had a major role in the story. The hero, of course, is Jesus, who played not only the part of God here on earth, but also my role. When He returned to heaven from His Palestinian years, He sent the third member of the Godhead to live in me the *very life* He had already lived in person on earth. That realization brought great rejoicing to me!

The everlasting covenant has two parts, God's and · man's. Jeremiah 32:38-40 is one of my favorite promises about the covenant:

> "They will be my people, and I will be their God. I will give them singleness of heart and action, so that they will always fear me for their own good and the good of their children after them. I will make an everlasting covenant with them: I will never stop doing good to them, and I will inspire them to fear me, so that they will never turn away from me."

As I progressed in my prayer walk I found that just as the eternal covenant has two parts, so does true prayer —God's part and my part. Prayer is the exercise of the covenant relationship with God.

Any in-depth study of the everlasting covenant leads to the need to understand more fully the closing work of Christ as our high priest in the heavenly sanctuary. Quickly I discovered that I had as many questions about this subject as I did about prayer.

Just what is it that God is doing up in heaven since 1844 that takes such a long time? Surely He has computers much more sophisticated than earthly ones and plenty of angel operators to perfectly feed in input and correlate output. He could know in an instant everything about the entire universe.

If the judgment exists in order for God to explain

something to the universe, then that might take a bit longer, limited, of course, by the capacity of created creatures to learn and understand. Still, they are *perfect* created beings, vastly more brilliant than humans and their computers. So if it isn't God or the universe who is holding up events, there is only one other plausible answer. It must have something to do with us. Do you suppose there might be something yet unfinished in heaven that needs completing, something going on simultaneously with and dependent upon earth happenings? Is it possible *I* might have anything to do with it?

One of the pillars upon which the pioneers of Seventh-day Adventism founded the church is the judgment-hour message. God's Word compared with world history shows that the message of the first angel of Revelation 14 began sounding in the late 1700s, preparing for the end of the 2300 day-prophecy in 1844. The work of the high priest in the Most Holy Place of the earthly sanctuary represents the final movements of earth's history. It's an impressive message, unusual, startling to the uninitiated, often made to look ridiculous and unchristian by other denominations. The major portion of Seventh-day Adventists understand it only in theory.

Theory ceased to satisfy me. I had to *know* what God was doing in the Most Holy Place in heaven. While I had read all the typical Adventist explanations, they left me unsatisfied.

One day I found a statement by Ellen White that said quite plainly that we should be willing to share with others the news of what Jesus is doing in the Most Holy Place during the period of the investigative judgment (see *Testimonies,* vol. 5, p. 575).

"I'd be glad to tell them," I sighed in despair, "if I knew what it was!"

Somehow I couldn't believe my neighbors would consider it good news that God was still at work on His books. There must be more to it.

I went at my investigation in my typical way, reading books, taking classes, questioning any friend or acquaintance who I suspected might have light on the subject. All to no avail. No one seemed to know any more than I did, and the intensity of my probing made people uneasy. It bothered me, too, that others did not seem to have the same urgent need to find the answer.

Consequently I slowed down my search. Perhaps I was going about it in the wrong way. It was about this time that my prayer group chose Jeremiah 33:3 as their theme promise. "Call to me," God says, "and I will answer you and tell you great and unsearchable things you do not know."

"God," I petitioned, "please show me what is going on in the investigative judgment. How can I tell others if *I* don't know myself? I long to be Your witness. Make me able to take my part in Your judgment message."

The experience with building our house and the uncertainty of not knowing where we were going to be living even a few weeks in the future, plus family and church problems, were such *immediate* issues that we had to deal with that I satisfied myself with just trying to get by each day. My utmost concern was that I assure myself that my relationship with Jesus was right *today*. Understanding the investigative judgment would have to wait for a more convenient time.

Delight and excitement now pervaded my prayer life as I learned to prevail with God in pushing back spiritual darkness and depression by confession and commitment. Because of my unsettled existence, I found God speaking to me particularly through some of the psalms.

> Blessed are those whose strength is in you,
>> who have set their hearts on *pilgrimage,*
> As they pass through the Valley of Baca,
>> they make it a place of springs;
>> the autumn rains also cover it with pools.
> They go from strength to strength,
>> till each appears before God in Zion (Psalm 84:5-7).

"Lord," I exclaimed, "I have set my heart on pilgrimage. May I go from strength to strength."

In spite of our unsettled living conditions, the Lord was extremely close to me at this time. For just a moment the impermanence of my life was almost exhilarating. Walking in such joy, I found it inconceivable that I would ever again dwell in darkness. Surely the Lord had shown me how to combat Satan's tricks in this area of my life, and I was ready with the weapons God had given me.

A Bible passage I should have had at the tip of my tongue is 1 Corinthians 10:12: "Wherefore let him that thinketh he standeth take heed lest he fall" (KJV). It is a verse Satan is well acquainted with, I'm sure. He hurled another family problem at me. In despair, because I could find no solution, I found myself hurtling into the blackest darkness of all.

I tried to pray through it—I truly did—but my words could not break through the accumulated gloom of guilt and fear. Panic-stricken, I found myself stuck in a never-never land of contagious fear. It was worse now than before I had learned to pray through emotional and spiritual darkness. If I failed now with all the knowledge God had given me and the beautiful experiences of the past to remember, then what hope was there for me?

God, in His great love and compassion, again used human agencies to reach me. A young Jewish man, Michael Curzon, was a member of our congregation. Only a few years before, he had been introduced to Jesus and had remained excited about it ever since. He had learned the Old Testament thoroughly as a boy and thus was familiar with the biblical accounts of the sanctuary services. Now, as a new Christian, he was amazed as he reviewed the history of his people. Everywhere he looked, he saw Jesus. In the Passover as practiced by devout Jews today he found Him. At the welcoming of the Sabbath at Friday sundown there was Jesus. In its observance he discovered Jesus. And in the Mosaic laws he met Jesus everywhere. "How have we missed seeing Him all these years?" Michael marveled.

Now, as a Seventh-day Adventist Christian, he determined to share the riches of the Old Testament laws and history in the revelation of Jesus. He had two favorite occupations. One was talking to others *about* Jesus, the other speaking *to* Him in prayer. His enthusiasm was boundless.

Michael had attracted my attention from our first meeting because he shared my love of prayer. However, I often found what he said confusing. Over the years I had laid aside my questions about the sanctuary, and here was Michael talking about it endlessly! When he preached I had a hard time understanding him. But his open love for Jesus warmed and touched my heart.

As I groped in the darkness surrounding me I clutched frantically at anything that promised hope. My daughter lent me a set of tapes of a seminar she had attended. Called *The Gospel in the Sanctuary,* it featured as speakers

Michael Curzon and Carol Zarska. Carol Zarska was a Bible worker and nurse from the East Coast who had found the study of the sanctuary just as fascinating as Michael had. She was a fourth-generation Adventist and Michael a converted Jew. What a combination! Only the Lord would have thought of putting the two together. It had been their first seminar together. Michael showed the gospel as revealed in the biblical sanctuary, while Carol presented the same message showing Jesus through the unique Seventh-day Adventist understanding.

As I listened to the tapes, not only was hope reborn in my heart, but I recognized immediately that Jesus was answering my years-ago prayer to understand the judgment. "Call to me and I will answer you and tell you great and unsearchable things you do not know" (Jeremiah 33:3). That promise was coming true!

Through all the turmoil I am relating to you, the Lord gave me strength and ability to help many others to study the Bible. My trust in God was always there. I relate these episodes from my life because I really believe that my inward struggles are not that rare. Many sincere Christians suffer through just such times alone, not knowing they have many brothers and sisters who could offer consolation and encouragement. I hope that my story will touch responsive chords in other hearts and lead them to persevere in a growing relationship with Jesus.

Every time the Lord Jesus has pulled me out of the pit of despair, I have discovered that I have fallen forward, and when He has set me once more upon my feet, I am much farther along the path than I was at the time I fell.

Summary

Prayer is the exercise of the covenant relationship with God. Its place in my life becomes plain as I study God's entire plan of redemption and view the whole picture revealed in the Bible. I can be confident that God is willing—yes, eager—to intervene in my life and the lives of those I pray for, as I read the Bible stories of just such intervention. Not only that, but God assures us that in the end He will eradicate sin. That is good news!

The best news yet—Jesus, as God, holds firmly one part of the covenant relationship, and the same Jesus, as man, grasps the other just as securely. Thus that covenant cannot be broken. God sends the third member of the Godhead to live in me the very life Jesus has already lived in person here on earth.

True prayer takes the Word of God and applies it to my life.

CHAPTER

6

Sanctuary Praying

Seventh-day Adventist teachings include the three angels' messages, the investigative judgment, and the sanctuary message. Our schools thoroughly indoctrinate our youth in such beliefs. Of course, that's good—it's always good to know truth. The only problem lies in the vast difference between truth in theory only and living truth that changes the life. Sometimes it almost seems as though learning the *theory* of truth indoctrinates a person *against* living truth.

If every teacher in our schools, every parent, every minister, anyone who taught truth in any way, had an *experience* in living truth, the problem would be solved. Then and then only could we effectively communicate such biblical concepts to the pupils. (Even in that case some would still be unable to accept it.) But how much greater would be the success of our educational system.

My understanding of what Jesus was doing in the Most Holy Place was elementary. I knew that in 1844 Jesus began to wind up the process of freeing our world from sin. He entered the Most Holy Place where heaven kept its records of every sin that any human being had ever committed. In 1844 Jesus Himself began investigating each individual, beginning with Adam and Eve, to see if each person has confessed every sin. If he or she has, He marks the individual "Saved." If a single unconfessed sin remains on one's record, that person's name is immediately blotted out of the book of life. As time progresses, Jesus will come to the names of those still living. When He reaches my name, my probation ends, and I am either saved or lost. After He has investigated every case, He will close the records and return to earth to collect those faithful to Him.

Put in a nutshell, that is what I believed. And it scared me. Naturally I did not want to think about it, for how could I possibly *know* if I'd confessed all my sins? In desperation I hoped that He didn't come to my name for a long time. Yes, I realized that Jesus died on the cross for the sins of the world, including mine. I knew that the blood of Jesus covered them. But my understanding of God's character led me to believe that my confession was the key to my receiving individual forgiveness. God would not force anyone to be forgiven. Oh, how I wished that He would send me a computer printout of my portion of the records so I could check to see if all my sins were confessed! It all seemed so *secretive*!

Yet over the years God has given me glimpses of His great plan. After all, He knew what I believed, every conflicting fragment of my beliefs, and He desired that I recognize the difference between theories and living truth. As I look back now I can see so plainly His leading.

Several years ago it really concerned me to find that sins I had thought I had long since overcome would sometimes crop back up in my life. Sometimes new ones that I had not even realized I had would appear. Other weaknesses in my life seemed hopeless to overcome. I feared I would always be deficient in those areas. One day, in abject despair, I poured out my heart to God.

"O Lord," I cried, "how can I possibly be ready for Your appearing?"

He responded to me through the words of James 1:2-4:

> Count it all joy, my brethren, when you meet various trials, for you know that the testing of your faith produces steadfastness. And let steadfastness have its full effect, that you may be perfect and complete, lacking in nothing (RSV).

"My dear Carrol," God added tenderly, "don't you see what you are doing? You are trying to take *My* work upon yourself. It is *My* responsibility to make you perfect, and *I promise to do so*. Trust Me. Your work is to yield wholly to My discipline, to rejoice in trials, to repent of every known sin, to cheerfully obey My words, and to cooperate fully with the Spirit in your life."

The load lifted from me was tremendous! How I rejoiced in the power and mercy of my Father. I could throw away the lists of sins to overcome and let God work on them in His way.

As I began listening to Michael and Carol's seminar on the gospel in the sanctuary, I remembered my prayer for understanding of the judgment. Now God was showing me the "great and unsearchable things" I did not know.

The first thing that struck me as I listened to the tapes was Michael's statement that he believed that God had set up *the sanctuary in the wilderness to represent how Christ saves each human soul*. It was an entirely new thought to me. I knew the Old Testament sanctuary services pointed forward to Christ, but the idea that they might have a personal meaning for *me* had never crossed my mind. Curzon went on to say that a year in the sanctuary service symbolized the entire lifeline of our earth. Thus we can discover just what Jesus is doing today by the Day of Atonement services, which represent heaven's final activity for our world.

Both Michael and Carol had discovered in the sanctuary services of the earthly tabernacle a pattern to aid in personal prayer. They believed the sanctuary services revealed the steps God uses to save each human being, and that by studying the steps we can learn to cooperate with God in His work for us. Both speakers had each begun using the steps the priests took daily in the sanctuary ritual as a form for their morning prayers, remembering that it is our privilege today to go every day with Jesus into the Holy of Holies. Thus by reverent preparation of their hearts they were ready to participate with Christ in the transformation He wanted to do in their lives.

Out of my darkness I saw an open door into the Most Holy Place in heaven where brightness unapproachable surrounded Jesus. The light from the open door reached out to me and Jesus held out His arms, calling, "Come."

As eagerly as I had begun the ABCs of prayer, I started praying through the sanctuary. You may think as you read this, *"Well, she just needed a crutch, but I don't."* And you may be right. I surely don't feel that in order to be saved we must use any one form of prayer. Yet I am glad to follow the map or guide that God places before me. Eager for salvation, I am willing to dip seven times in a muddy river if that is what I feel He is asking of me.

It was exciting news to find that the work of investigation that Jesus was doing now was not an impersonal study of the records of heaven but a searching of *my* heart and life. The record of *my* sins defiles the courts above. Jesus, with His open arms, was eager to show me what was written about me in the heavenly books. In His love and mercy He wasn't content to just hand me a written printout of the gruesome details. Oh no, He would deal with me patiently. Point by point He would show me what existed in the unclean depths of my heart. From the moment of my birth He had been examining my name. Having no desire to keep any of His dealings secret from me, He wanted to *reveal* to me right now the deepest parts of my heart and mind. With my willing cooperation, He would purify me so that I could quit sinning, even unconsciously. Then He could remove my sins forever from the heavenly records. He promises to expose the root sins that cause my sinful acts so that I can *fully repent.* Thus, even sinful tendencies I was born with, those my parents had given me by birth, could be eliminated. Joy filled my soul as I, for the first time in my life, began to understand and appreciate the three angels' messages. Now I am ready to tell my neighbors what Jesus is doing in the Most Holy Place.

As I looked back on my life I could see that God had long been doing His work for me, although I had not understood it clearly before. Now I could cooperate with Him and was eager to begin.

My prayer life brightened immediately. No matter what problems engulf me I can relive in my mind the steps taken in the sanctuary service—praise to God as I enter into worship; repentance, confession, and forgiveness at the bronze altar (representing the cross of Jesus); cleansing and renewal at the laver of baptism; the outpouring of the Holy Spirit for my daily needs at the lampstand; and strength and daily sustenance at the table of the bread of His presence. Thus I am prepared for intercessory praying at the altar of incense. Having such a mental framework makes it possible for me to keep even a harried mind on prayer.

In the Most Holy Place I encounter the special judgment work Jesus wants to do for His people right now, digging down to the motives, attitudes, and root sins, both inherited and cultivated, beneath the common everyday sins that so often overtake me.

The investigative judgment is not just a secret examination of the heavenly records. Jesus seeks to enlist my cooperation in *removing* my sins. He wants to show me what those records contain so that I can repent and be healed. I'll admit the healing sometimes hurts, but oh the joy of finding healing possible. In a way it's like having a splinter taken out. It hurts in the removal, but it feels so good to begin to heal.

Jeremiah 30:12 tells it like it is: "This is what the Lord says: 'Your wound is incurable, your injury beyond healing.' " But in verse 17 the prophet gives the almost unbelievable good news:

" 'But I will restore you to health and heal your wounds.' "

Summary

The sanctuary system set up in the wilderness is a vital part of salvation. *By it God has represented how He saves each human being.* Rather than keeping His records, plans, and work secret, God desires to reveal them to every seeking heart.

We can cooperate with God in His work of revelation and cleansing by reliving daily in our minds the steps the earthly priests took in their sanctuary work.

1. Praise to God as we enter His courts by faith.

2. Repentance, confession, and forgiveness at the bronze altar, representing the cross of Christ.

3. Cleansing and daily renewal at the laver of baptism.

4. Outpouring of the Holy Spirit for our daily needs at the lampstand.

5. Strength and daily sustenance at the table of the bread of His presence.

6. Preparation to pray for others at the altar of incense.

7. In the Most Holy Place, allowing God to dig down

to our motives, attitudes, and root sins, both inherited and cultivated.

Don't expect it to be easy—it is never easy to overcome self. That is a fact that every Christian learns. But, praise God, He gives us the victory.

CHAPTER

7

Great and Unsearchable Things

It is one thing to bring before the Lord each morning and evening repentance for sins committed and to ask Him for guidance in every area of your life, but it is something else entirely to deliberately entreat the Lord to dig down into your heart and dredge up what you may well wish to remain hidden. Even things you had no idea were there!

Yet that was the step I took when I began "sanctuary praying." At first I didn't realize, of course, the magnitude of what I was beginning. I couldn't know that once I started on the serious business of cooperating fully with God in His investigation of my heart, I would never be the same again. Also, that I would never, never want to go back—not even to the occasional days when I seemed to walk in God's open presence. You see, I was now confident that He was steadily continuing the transformation in me that would be complete only on the day of Christ's appearing (Philippians 1:6).

Now I could know that even on the days when everything seemed to go wrong God's work in me was still going forward. More and more He can share His secrets with me, and more and more I can represent Him in the world. By this I do not mean that I am getting better and better. If anything, I seem, to myself at least, to be getting worse and worse. (Actually, I am for the first time in my life seeing myself as I really am!) But my *hope* is becoming stronger and stronger, because I know my salvation does not depend upon how good I am but solely upon the faithfulness of God. I must trust Him to complete the task He has begun in me.

One of my first questions to God in the Most Holy Place was "Lord, why can't You make me perfect all at once? Why does it take so long?" After all, the Bible does say that we become new creatures with new hearts as soon as we are born again. And we do. We have new motives, new loves, new joys. Because God has our will, we *will* to serve Him. But the Lord decided long ago that He would never force any creature to obey Him. Love is the *only* force that He will use. If God is going to have a universe full of perfect reasoning creatures to interact with Him throughout eternity, they are going to have to have had a choice at every step of their character building.

In these final days of the investigative judgment, the work in our hearts will intensify as God prepares a significant group of people who will perfectly reveal Him to the world.

The Lord was calling me to be an active participant in severe reforms in my life. So often we see clearly the faults of others, while our own, so familiar and, in many cases, so *dear,* we totally overlook or minimize. The cutting away of lifelong habits may, in fact, make us fear for our identity.

Each of us has worked out, over time, the way we deal

with life. All of us have found ways to escape when pressure gets too great. Some of them may be good, but many are only retreats from reality.

As a little child, I had found that when unpleasantness or boredom threatened me, I could make up harmless little stories of pleasant things and pleasant places. Later, as I learned to read, storybooks served the same purpose. If life grew too burdensome, complex, or depressing, I retreated into them.

When I chose Christianity during my teen years, I began to recognize the dangers in my habit. However, in my zealousness I completely cut out all daydreaming and storybook reading from my life and discovered that I had unwanted and unasked-for companions—resentment and self-pity. I experienced more difficulty eliminating them by willpower than I did daydreaming and novel reading. So I worked out a compromise that I considered good Christian living. From now on I would daydream only good things. Thus I redecorated houses in my mind, made trips, imagined what I'd do if someone gave me a million dollars, etc.

Knowing they were sinful, I rejected romantic dreams of obvious aggrandizement of self. For my reading, I chose good moral novels or historical adventure. Thus I worked out a life I could live with. At the same time I studied the Bible and prayed earnestly, and God blessed me in the Christian walk. Sometimes I could go weeks or months with no need for my special retreats. But they were always available.

As I began praying with the judgment specifically in mind, I asked God to purify the roots of sin from my life. I suspected that the Lord would have to deal with my escapist pattern of life. And He did not disappoint me.

The Lord speaks to us in many ways. As we read Scripture we often hear His voice. Nature reminds us of His care, and sometimes we hear His voice in particular instruction for us in the things He has made. Often He leads our contemplative thoughts to dwell on Him. But occasionally He interjects Bible verses, songs, poetry, or statements into our thinking in a new and arresting way that cannot be mistaken for happenstance.

As I began praying, using the earthly sanctuary as a metaphor of Christ's work for me in the heavenly sanctuary, I began listening carefully for His voice to me, expecting to hear it first as I symbolically prayed in the Most Holy Place. But who can explain His ways? He chose to speak to me most often as I went about my work around the house.

One morning as I arose from my prayer and stood in the middle of the room that I used as my morning chapel, God reminded me that if I am talking on the telephone and someone needs to reach me, that person can call the operator and ask for an emergency interruption to my call. We have had that happen to us, so I was well aware of the possibility. Then the Lord went on to say through His Spirit that He doesn't operate that way. If my mental line is busy, He can't reach me. I am always free to choose to hear Him or not. It is my decision alone.

It was an interesting thought, but not exactly how I had pictured that God would begin to deal with me. I wondered what its significance was. Somehow it didn't seem very personal.

The next week, Wednesday morning, while I was doing the breakfast dishes I heard His voice again.

"Theirs not to reason why, theirs but to do and die."

At first I thought the line must be a Bible verse He was

bringing to my mind, as this is often the way the Lord speaks. However, upon reflection, I recognized it as obviously a line from a dimly remembered poem. God went on to say that unreasoning obedience is what the world seeks—*blind* obedience. But He desires only *intelligent* response. It is all right to question God, because He wants us to understand and welcomes our questions. He has made us rational creatures, and it is through our reasoning power that He communicates to us.

Then God continued by explaining that novel reading and daydreaming are so destructive because they block our channel of communication to God so that He cannot speak to us. Our reasoning centers are occupied with escapist thoughts.

"But God," I countered, "we all have a physical life to live. We have to put our minds to the stretch, making a living, cooking, sewing, driving, working out complicated problems. How can we be thinking about You all the time?"

"My child," He gently answered, *"whenever your reasoning powers are working, the line to me is open. It is when reason has vacated the mind that it closes."*

Through my mind flashed a list of similar obstructions to reason: alcohol, drugs of any sort, TV, frivolity, self-pity, jealousy, anger, hypnosis, rock music, resentment, lust—and many more.

Immediately I was convinced. God had gently but firmly begun dealing with the unsearchable things hidden in my heart. They would remain concealed no longer.

Later research revealed that the line "Theirs not to reason why, theirs but to do and die" came from "The Charge of the Light Brigade," by Alfred, Lord Tennyson. The poem had been a favorite of my father, and he had often repeated it to me when I was a child. It is the story of a battalion of soldiers who charged the enemy at the orders of their commander even though they realized it would mean certain death. Their military training had instilled in them an unreasoning obedience. God had used this small fragment of verse, stored away in my mind, to show me the contrast between His concept of obedience and that of the world.

I was elated. The ax was at the root of the tree. Wanting nothing more than to please God, I confessed my sins and felt sure that I would be walking in the sunlight continually until Jesus comes. Later I shared my experience with our small prayer group and a larger one that met at our house on Friday nights.

Now that God had revealed to me exactly how dangerous my lifelong pattern of escapism was and I had confessed my sinfulness to Him, romantic that I am, I felt sure the problem was behind me. Little did I understand the extent of sin in my life or how interwoven sin's tendrils become in all areas of our lives. I felt sure that God had reached into the bottom of my heart and shown me the root of all my sinning. After all, I had confessed it. Surely that would be the end of the matter. All would now be easy.

In actuality it was only the beginning. God was first cleaning out my line to Him. The rest would follow.

Summary

Sanctuary praying—in prayer following the steps of the priests in the earthly sanctuary—means cooperating fully with God in His investigation of our hearts.

The only force God ever uses is love. Human beings remain free at every step of their lifewalk to choose either Christ or self. Such daily choices determine our character development. More and more clearly God will reveal to us their results. And more and more clearly we will be able to distinguish the voice of God. God desires not blind obedience, but an intelligent choice to serve Him in every particular. We should remove from our lives any habit or pastime that does not involve reason.

8

The Night
Shall Be Light

It brought me great joy when, with the aid of confession and commitment, I pushed through anything that seemed to block my prayer time. Coupled with sanctuary praying, it ushered in a totally new era for my morning devotions. Daily I praised God for His growing blessings.

However, I encountered another sort of darkness that seemed impenetrable by my prayers. It usually followed a time when I strongly doubted my own sincerity. Perhaps I had sinned, either deliberately or just from habit. Or another family problem had just fallen upon my head. Often it was a combination of both.

One Sunday especially stands out in my memory. I had been caught in the downward spiral of spiritual depression for several days. My Sabbath school class and nearly all of my individual Bible studies had canceled out. It was as though God had no need for me any longer. Family problems loomed heavily over me. Because I knew that the Bible plainly says that "God is light; in Him there is no darkness at all" (1 John 1:5), I concluded that when darkness hung all about me like it did then, it surely meant that somehow I had left Him behind. I knew God never turned away from me, for He "does not change like shifting shadows" (James 1:17), so I must have been the one who had abandoned Him.

That Sunday I went to the swap meet with my husband and wandered disconsolately up and down the aisles. Unable to generate any interest in any of the displays, I soon returned to the car to await John's return. I could think of nothing but my loneliness for God.

In desperation I took my little Bible out of my purse and pleaded, "O Lord, please speak to me someway through Your Word. Is there no way back to You?" I opened the Bible at random, and the following passage caught my attention:

> "Can a mother forget the baby at her breast
> and have no compassion on the child she has borne?
> Though she may forget,
> I will not forget you!
> See, I have engraved you on the palms of my hands" (Isaiah 49:15, 16).

"O God!" I cried as humility, thankfulness, and joy rushed through my being. "Please forgive me for doubting. How could I have doubted? You will never forget me. You have engraved me upon the palms of Your hands." Then I read the rest of the chapter, blessed and fed by the Word of God.

"You know," God continued, "I was there even in the darkness."

"You were?" I breathed, astonished at the thought. "You were there in the darkness? But in You there is no darkness at all. How could it be?"

"I'm just as close to you in the darkness as in the light. It's all the same to Me."

"All the same?"

"Yes," He answered.

And then I remembered a psalm I had memorized. How could I have not realized what it meant?

> Where can I go from your Spirit?
> > Where can I flee from your presence?
> If I go up to the heavens, you are there;
> > if I make my bed in the depths, you are there.
> If I rise on the wings of the dawn,
> > if I settle on the far side of the sea,
> even there your hand will guide me,
> > your right hand will hold me fast.

> If I say, "Surely the darkness will hide me
> > and the light become night around me,"
> even the darkness will not be dark to you;
> > the night will shine like the day;
> > for darkness is as light to you (Psalm 139:7-12).

Joy eddied around me the rest of the day. Every now and then I would ask again, "You really were there all the time?"

"Yes."

"You are *always* with me in *all* my darknesses?"

"Yes. I will *never* leave you nor forsake you."

"Then why the darkness, Lord?" Finally I could ask that question.

"My child," He spoke in tones of tenderness, "now is the time to prepare you for eternity. *The darkness is necessary in order to burn out sin.*"

"But You're always there," I questioned again, "even in the darkness?"

"Always."

"O my Father," I responded, "now that I know You are always with me, I don't mind dwelling in the darkness. I'm content to remain there *with You* until You come in the clouds of heaven."

But the darkness had fled away, and it was bright with the presence of God.

Later, as I was doing the dishes, a biblical assurance flashed into my mind:

> Whatever they plot against the Lord
>   he will bring to an end;
> trouble will not come the second time (Nahum 1:9).

"Lord, that's a promise for the end of sin in the *world,*" I argued. "It's not meant for an individual."

"It's a promise for *you,*" God reiterated. "If you are faithful, there will be an end of sin in your life. And trouble will not come a second time. It's My promise to you."

The next morning I was doing the dishes when I again heard His voice.

"Would you like to know *why* you dwell in the darkness so much?"

"Yes, Lord, if You want to tell me."

"It's because you don't trust Me."

A few hours later a young woman I love very much unloaded a barrage of bitterness upon me. Immediately and distinctly I heard the voice of God.

"Well, are you going to trust her with Me or are you going into the darkness?"

"O Lord," I breathed, "she's Yours. Take this dear one of mine and deal with her as You do with me. I trust You to care for her."

Later I realized that the little incident was exactly the

sort of thing that usually triggered my descents into spiritual depression. God had kindly shown me exactly how it always happened. I shouldn't be surprised, though, for He has promised to do just that:

> O people of Zion, who live in Jerusalem, you will weep no more. How gracious he will be when you cry for help! As soon as he hears, he will answer you. Although the Lord gives you the bread of adversity and the water of affliction, *your teachers will be hidden no more;* with your own eyes you will see them. Whether you turn to the right or to the left, your ears will hear a voice behind you, saying, "This is the way; walk in it" (Isaiah 30:19-21).

And so you see, though I had fallen into spiritual darkness and depression through lack of trust, yet when God rescued me from the pit I was far, far ahead of where I had been standing when I stumbled. That is part of God's precious plan for our sanctification. He can use even our failures as a step forward and upward.

Summary

Spiritual darkness, or depression, does not indicate that God has withdrawn His presence from us. He will never leave us nor forsake us. Sometimes, though, He will allow His face to be hidden from us so that we may learn to trust Him more fully. As a plant grows even in the darkness, so we grow by trusting God explicitly in the dark times of our lives.

God desires to teach us how to trust Him in every particular of our lives. He seeks to show us the inner workings of our hearts and minds. Through repentence, God uses even our failures as steps toward heaven.

Bible verses that have helped me to endure the dark times:

Psalm 139:7-12
Psalm 23:4

9

Prayer Places and Times

Have you noticed how often the kitchen sink has entered my story? Well, perhaps not by name, but surely by implication. Although the living room is my morning prayer room, my kitchen holds countless memories of conversations with Jesus. Many of the greatest insights and much of the instruction the Holy Spirit has impressed upon my mind have come as I worked there, often while doing the dishes.

But dishwashing was the bane of my childhood. I hated doing dishes. Oh, occasionally my sisters and I had good times together as we washed the dishes, but more often than not we argued about who was doing the most work. Now I realize that I carried resentment over it into my adult life, and He has asked me to let it go. You see, I was not only the middle daughter but the sickly one as well. Because I was unable to do the heavy outdoor chores that country living demanded, dishwashing was a suitable responsibility. Mother never asked me to do them alone. Childlike, I did not realize that the outdoor work both my sisters did more than balanced the extra dishes I did.

God's goodness amazes me as I realize that He has taken one of the plague spots in my life and made it a channel of communication with Him. Sometimes I find myself even anticipating running the hot water into the sink, pouring in the soap, and watching the bubbles spring up. As I plunge the dirty dishes into the water, it reminds me of the fountain that God has prepared for *my* cleansing. Perhaps that is why He has chosen the kitchen sink as a special place of revelation for me.

Let me relive a few memories from the kitchen sink.

In the days when we lived in the big house that we had built and were preparing to sell it to begin our lives anew, I tried hard to anticipate what God's plans were for our future. One of my favorite occupations was daydreaming about how He could work it out for us. (It was before He pointed out to me the consequences of daydreaming.) One afternoon while washing dishes at the kitchen sink, I gazed at the splendor of the distant mountains and imagined a fantastic way that God could resolve our troubles. Very clearly He interrupted my thoughts.

"Carrol," He said, "I don't want you to even try to imagine what I am going to do for you." Those words stopped me abruptly in the middle of my daydream. "Yes, Lord," came my obedient response. Since that time, often when I seek to anticipate what God is going to do, He reminds me of that afternoon at the kitchen sink. Now I realize that He is seeking to create in me a *trust* that will leave it all in His hands. I don't have to know all the answers.

Another house, another kitchen, another sink. We sold the big house and moved into another lovely home that we knew would be only a temporary abode until our finances straightened out. In this house my kitchen window did not open out upon faraway vistas but upon a private garden of quiet loveliness. As I looked out I saw the soft blending of shadows and sunlight, the sparkling blue of a swimming pool, and the vibrant colors of flowers. Once I had watched out that window as a mother hummingbird hatched her perfect little eggs. It was at this same sink that God told me about the harmfulness of daydreaming and novel reading. But it is another incident that I want to recount now.

Life was again in the midst of a tremendous muddle for me. At the slightest provocation depression and spiritual darkness seemed to drape over me like a curtain. (That was before God told me He was always there in the darkness.) I had been sick with a bad cold and welcomed a couple of days of quietness. Sabbath came and I read and slept and prayed the morning away. My husband arrived home from church and relaxed in one of the rockers in our bedroom to relay church news to me. We were in no hurry for lunch. I was not very hungry, and since I had not prepared any food for Sabbath, my husband would have to fend for himself.

The doorbell rang. As I listened from upstairs, John answered the door. Friends from San Diego had dropped in unexpectedly. My husband brought them up the stairs to greet me and then suggested to Dona, the wife, that she help him fix some lunch. So together the three of them went down to the kitchen. Quickly dressing, I joined them.

We had just finished lunch when our daughter, Julie, her husband, Andy, and the two little granddaughters showed up. Eventually we migrated to the living room, where I curled up on the couch while everyone visited. The kitchen scene kept intruding in the back of my

Martha mind. The table had not been cleaned up, the dishes not even removed from the table. But it was not my affair. I was sick.

The afternoon passed quickly. We had sundown worship together, and then our San Diego friends departed. The little girls began suggesting supper. No one made a move toward the kitchen. Unwelcome thoughts crept into my mind. "Surely they don't expect *me* to fix a meal for them all? I'm sick!" And I remembered the state of the kitchen.

Finally I pulled myself from the couch. Unbelievable chaos reigned in the kitchen. The dishwasher hung open and all kinds of debris hid the table. Wearily I scraped food off plates into the garbage disposal, rinsed them, and filled the dishwasher. All the while I could hear the others laughing in the living room. Running hot water into the sink, I added detergent to finish up the dishes I could not put into the dishwasher. All this time my busy mind was racing with resentment, self-pity, and anger.

"I suppose I'll have to fix supper for them all when I finish the cleanup," I muttered to myself, "and I'm sick!"

"You don't have to think these thoughts." Abruptly I stopped.

"What?" I exclaimed.

"You don't have to think these thoughts." I knew it was the voice of God interrupting my self-pitying tirade. But what He said was true. I could *choose* not to think such destructive thoughts. Joy and peace filled my heart. Quickly finishing the dishes, I returned to the family room couch and watched as my husband, our daughter, and her husband popped corn, made sandwiches, and prepared fruit for supper. Martha-me had wanted everything done quickly and in my timing. But when I sat back, the others went into action and everyone had a good time.

"Thank You, Lord, for Your intervention in my life."

God still reminds me on other appropriate occasions, "You don't have to think these thoughts," and I relive that evening. I set my will in action, and God changes my thoughts from self-pity, criticism, or anger to ones of peace, joy, and contentment.

While in the process of unraveling our financial affairs we made another move, this time into a temporary rental. Nearly two years later we are still here. My kitchen window here does not look out either on distant mountains or on a lovely inner garden. Yet God has blessed me with a bougainvillea vine that hangs over the fence from the neighboring yard and fills my kitchen window with bright beauty. It makes me smile whenever I walk in the front door and meet that blaze of color. (Three things warm up my life: an open fire on a cold day, the beauty of color any day, and an honest smile directed my way.)

When God rebuked me for daydreaming and novel reading, I never planned to resume such practices. Yet there seemed to be such a void in my life without them. They have always been such a *comfort* to me. When I first voiced my sense of emptiness to the Lord, He assured me that He would fill up that void with His Spirit. And He has. But at times I have longed for the familiar comfort of reading and dreaming.

One morning as I talked with God during my morning prayer time God spoke to me through 2 Corinthians 1:3, 4:

> Praise be to the God and Father of our Lord Jesus
>   Christ, the Father of compassion and the
> God of all comfort, who comforts us in all our
>   troubles, so that we can comfort those
> in any trouble with the comfort we ourselves have received.

"I want to be all comfort to you," He said. "You need nothing more than Me." For days that warmed my heart.

I have a little shop in an antique mall where I sell dolls, books, and various other old things. It brings me in a little money for extras, and I enjoy the social contact and variety the little business adds to my life.

One day my husband stopped by a thrift shop and purchased several old books that he thought I might like to sell in *my* shop. As I was getting ready to eat my lunch alone the next day I picked up one of the books to browse through it. Inside the musty-looking cover the pages were quaintly old-fashioned, and I was curious about what they contained, though I did not expect to really read the book. It was old and no doubt boring, and I began to suspect it was a novel. But as I browsed through it I became involved with the story plot. Before I realized it, I was hooked. Sadly I looked at it, knowing that in my weakness I was sure to finish reading it. At first I tried to justify myself with the thought that since it was such an old book, surely it was all right to read it. Then I remembered Ellen White's comments about the addiction of novel reading and realized this might have been one of the very books that she cautioned against. With regret I put a marker in my place as I finished my lunch, knowing that even though I didn't want to disappoint Jesus, yet because of my weakness, I would surely read it. It had happened so often before in spite of all my good resolutions. As I arose from the table I began talking with Jesus.

"You know, Lord, that I can put the book away now, or even dispose of it, yet I'll fail again another time. Lord, what can I do? I want to be through with this in my life."

Into my mind came a phrase from *Steps to Christ* in which Mrs. White mentions one who has confessed his sins; and "in heart put them away" (p. 49).

"My Father," I asked, "how can I put this away?"

"Pull out the marker," came the direct answer.

Obediently I did so. Now the book did not look ready to read. As I began washing the lunch dishes I reviewed the incident in my mind. Suddenly the story plot gripped me again, and I had an overwhelming desire to finish the book. In fact, I wanted to read it immediately. Removing my hands from the soapy water to reach for it, I heard my lips utter aloud, "No!" and the temptation faded. As far as I could tell, the word was involuntary. Not my conscious mind, but something deep within me responded to the temptation. Instantly I remembered that Ellen White says in *The Desire of Ages* that the expulsion of sin from the heart is the work of the soul itself.

> In the work of redemption there is no compulsion. No external force is employed. Under the influence of the Spirit of God, man is left free to choose whom he will serve. In the change that takes place when the soul surrenders to Christ, there is the highest sense of freedom. The expulsion of sin is the act of the soul itself. True, we have no power to free ourselves from Satan's control; but when we desire to be set free from sin, and in our great need cry out for a power out of and above ourselves, the powers of the soul are imbued with the divine energy of the Holy Spirit, and they obey the dictates of the will in fulfilling the will of God (p. 466).

Twice more in the next 15 minutes I had this same experience.

Is it any wonder that my kitchen seems to me to be a place of prayer, or dishwashing a part of worship? There the miracle of renewal, in object lesson and in my heart, takes place daily.

Summary

Sometimes God will take an area of our lives that has caused us much bitterness and resentment and turn it into a special blessing. He has done that with me with housework, especially the times when I am washing the dishes. The Lord has chosen a daily task, dishwashing, and the common place, the kitchen sink, to commune with me.

Some of the principles He has shared there with me are:

1. He wants me to leave my future entirely in His hands and not have things so minutely planned that it is hard for me to see what He desires for me.

2. The Lord has given each of us freedom to choose the thoughts that will occupy our minds. I can *choose* to think only positive thoughts.

3. Surrendering my soul to God brings true freedom from sin. I will then even involuntarily say "No!" to sin.

<u>10</u>

Bible Study
in Prayer

It is impossible to keep alive a relationship with Jesus without much Bible study. So many of us go at Bible study in a haphazard way, thus often receiving little benefit. True Bible study is a science that dedicated seekers for truth should eagerly cultivate.

I have mentioned in an earlier chapter how the everlasting covenant theme tied the entire Bible together and made it more understandable to me. Many other themes will produce similar results. Ellen White talks often of the great controversy or struggle between Christ and Satan. A friend of mine relates every vital issue of life to one of the three crosses on Calvary. To everyone who searches the Bible by the power of the Holy Spirit God will give a greater grasp of the Scriptures.

I often had difficulty with Bible texts that I felt contradicted each other. It seemed impossible for me with my limited intelligence to understand such a diverse book. Then one day the Lord helped me to realize that divine things can never be perfectly explained in human words. Unless the Spirit of God is present as we read, we will only become confused. I caught a glimpse of how limited human beings are in their understanding of God. Even if Jesus Himself were here to explain heavenly things in the best human words possible, without the aid of the Holy Spirit they would be incomprehensible to all of us.

When Jesus lived here upon earth as a man, He sought to open human minds to the reality of divine things. He said, "I am the way, the truth, and the life." "I am the good shepherd." "I am the door." "I am the light of the world." "I am the bread of life." Yet none of these things is similar to each other. Light is nothing like bread, nor is a door like a shepherd. God is saying, Don't be bound by any one thing in your understanding of Me. Open up your minds and allow heavenly concepts to fill and expand your thoughts. God is larger than you imagine.

Now when I find a Bible verse that seems to contradict my understanding of other biblical teachings, I stop to consider that either I am misinterpreting that particular verse or my concept of the entire teaching is too narrow, or even mingled with error. My next step is a prayer for wisdom and comprehension (a prayer God delights to answer!), and then I wait for God to respond to that prayer in His own time.

By waiting for God's timing I do not mean I stop studying the Bible, or even the subject in question. Decidedly not! But I do cease *worrying* about it. Perhaps not everyone has the same difficulty I have, but I tend to become irrational when I start worrying. Satan has so many clever traps to try and keep us from getting to know God, and worry is one of his favorites. With worry out of the way I am free to hear the voice of God as I go about my studying. I make no demands of Him, knowing that He will show me truth as I am ready for it. Instead I just want to do my best to be constantly stretching my mind toward Him.

Occasionally it has been imperative that I grasp a certain subject by a specific time, as I have to *teach* it to someone else. In that case I ask the Lord for special wisdom and state my problem. "O Lord," I cry, "if You don't show me truth, I will teach error. Lead me in the path of truth. I need Your special revelation." God has always proved Himself faithful to me. Sometimes His answer is that I should simply state what I have been sure of for many years and then acknowledge that I do not know the rest. Humbling, perhaps, but so much better than presumption.

I know of only one way to learn to love Bible study. The first step is to love Jesus, the author of the Bible. The next step is nearly as important, becaues it ensures the maintenance of a love relationship between you and Jesus: read the Bible every day. Spend time with the Word. Claim scriptural promises as you pray. Memorize Bible passages. Talk about it to others. In summary, immerse yourself in the Word.

This step may sound easy but it is not. Satan does not desire anyone to read the Bible and will devise countless distractions to keep you from its study.

I have talked before about the importance of a regular morning time with God for prayer and Bible study. In order to learn to love the Bible, one has to study the Word more than once a day. Therefore I suggest an evening period for more leisurely reading. Since so many people ask *how* to begin studying the Bible, I would like to mention some of the principles that work for me. They are not original with me. Many other Christians have aided me in learning how to study Scripture.

The first principle is to petition the Lord to fill you with the Holy Spirit as you begin, a prayer that the Lord delights to answer. He will give you the humble spirit of the learner as you open the pages of the Holy Book.

One method of Bible study is to choose a topic or subject and with the help of a concordance find a number of texts on that subject. The center references in many Bibles aid in such an investigation. Often, too, as you become more and more familiar with the pages of the Bible, God Himself will bring to your mind other passages. Such an approach resembles a treasure hunt and has all sorts of exciting possibilities. It is well to document your study by writing down the subject and the texts discovered. You might even want to link the texts together in your Bible for easy finding to share with others.

One caution, though: be sure to read each passage in its context. Read the verses before and after it. If it is part of a story, become acquainted with the entire narrative. Do not be too hasty in your conclusions. Take time to learn. Often the stories of the Bible will give you as much spiritual help as individual verses do. Should you find you don't get far on your study in the time you have allotted yourself, you may need to set aside a longer space of time tomorrow. Do not become discouraged, though, with even brief study periods. God can teach you amazing things in a short span. Be sure to allow yourself time to contemplate the verses you have read and their relationship to your own life. If your study time is just before you go to sleep, you may find the quiet time after you are in bed most useful for this. By making your final thoughts of the day of Jesus, you will find your first thoughts in the morning are likely to be of Him, also.

Another method for Bible study is to read whole

chapters, perhaps the best way to begin. Our small group studied the Gospel of John chapter by chapter. All the way through our church schools my teachers had taught me to approach the Bible in a topical manner. Thus it was the method I understood best. Yet now I found that reading whole chapters and applying them to myself personally brought new life to my Bible study habits. Topical study is fascinating in its discovery, but chapter-by-chapter reading is more apt to reach the heart of scripture.

I will include some of the principles we used in our examination of the book of John. First we read the chapter through together, each member of our group taking a few verses. Then we discussed the setting of the chapter and the characters involved in each episode. In order to personalize the material we questioned just who each person in the chapter represents. For example, Jesus always depicts God and the sinner represents us. Sometimes we were the disciples, sometimes the scribes and Pharisees, other times the individual healed. Often we saw ourselves in the most unlovely of the characters. We noticed the way Jesus dealt with that person, and we thanked God that He would approach us that way, too. Then we sought to establish the theme of the chapter by looking for words that appear again and again. Our group watched for comparisons and contrasts in actions, attitudes, and characters. And we noticed any illustrations given in the chapter. If reference was made to an account in the Old Testament, we went back and reread the story and discussed why the chapter alluded to it. Each Bible study session was a look into our own hearts.

I think of such Bible study as a fomentation treatment. As the hot fomentation loosens congestion in the body, so heartfelt Bible study breaks up the grip of sin on us. And as a cold fomentation must follow a hot one to protect against further congestion, so prayers for forgiveness for the past and commitment for the future must accompany each Bible study. In fact, if you are studying alone or in a small group, whenever the chapter gives the opportunity for you to make a commitment, pause right then and do it. Never pass by an opportunity to renew or deepen your dedication to Jesus. Thus your Bible study time can be a prayer session, too.

Sometimes, I'll have to admit, I have found the Bible boring, dry, and uninteresting. In fact, it often seemed that way to me in the beginning of my quest for God. I enjoyed reading books *about* the Bible more than I did the actual reading of the Word.

But one of my first prayers during the early days of my search for meaning in my life was, "Lord, teach me to love Your Word."

Now that kind of love doesn't spring up fully grown. One evening I heard a well-known evangelist tell the story of his mother and her love for her Bible. "I have often seen my mother lift her Bible to her lips and kiss it. How she loved it!" he told us.

Squirming in my seat, I thought, *What a sentimental little old lady his mother must be. Imagine kissing a Bible.* And I inwardly laughed.

The years flew by, and I spent much time with my Bible. Even more than truth, I found there God's compassion and mercy for a sinner like me. I memorized, I underlined, I highlighted, I read and shared with others. Tears fell on my Bible as I prayed over its open pages.

Then came a day not too long ago when I was cleaning house. As I hurried from room to room I spotted my well-worn red Bible lying on a table. Smiling, I quickly reached out and patted it, one, two, three times as I passed by. I stopped abruptly as the story of the old woman kissing her Bible flashed into my mind. Were love pats much different from kisses?

My young love had grown and spread and mellowed until it flowed out of my fingertips. I had found in my Bible a love letter from God. But that isn't the end. The years of eternity as they roll by will only add to my love for my then-seen God.

No, love doesn't spring up fully grown. The beginning of love is just the promise of loving for eternity.

These three never fail: faith, hope, and love. And we uncover all three through study of the Word of God. All three are revealed in Jesus.

Summary

S pecific things that have helped my Bible study are:

1. Asking for the guidance of the Holy Spirit.
2. Reading the Bible every day.
    a. Early-morning time daily.
    b. Evening time for more reading and contemplation.
    c. Both topical (by subject) and the reading of entire chapters and books. The more you read the Bible, the more you will love it!
3. Searching for the theme that runs throughout the Bible and making it one story.
4. Avoiding preconceived ideas.
5. Being willing to wait for any complete understanding of many subjects.
6. Putting Bible principles into practice. Act them out in daily life.
7. Asking myself what this tells me about the character of God. Do not just fill your mind with Bible facts, but seek to know God better.

11

More,
Much More

Every new revelation from God has thrilled me. Each one has been like a present, wrapped up and handed to me by God. I would take time unwrapping it, fondle and caress it, and then put it away in the back of my mind to pull out and look at every day or so. I would think sweet thoughts of Jesus, how I loved Him, and how I appreciated the gifts He had given me. Each gift satisfied me for a long time. I would not be so greedy as to ask for more!

Then one day God revealed to me a new glimpse of Himself. Actually, He showed me something about myself and then asked me if I thought He was less than that.

One of our family's summer favorites is homemade peach ice cream. Eagerly we share our specialty with guests, watching expectantly as they take the first bite.

"Good," they may murmur politely. Or some may even exclaim, "Delicious!" But the real test comes when they have finished the small bowlful and we ask tentatively, "Would you like some more?"

Now, some say politely, "No, thanks; that was delicious, but I've had enough." We look sideways at each other, feeling disappointment that our guests cannot share the delight of peach ice cream with us.

But some comment, "Now that's what ice cream should taste like! Delicious! Can I have some more?"

With delight we fill their bowls up to the brim. Our own ice cream tastes better because they are sharing with us in this special experience.

One day I read the story in *The Desire of Ages* of Jesus at the wedding feast. The following passage intrigued me:

> The gifts of Jesus are ever fresh and new. The feast that He provides for the soul never fails to give satisfaction and joy. Each new gift increases the capacity of the receiver to appreciate and enjoy the blessings of the Lord. He gives grace for grace. There can be no failure of supply. If you abide in Him, the fact that you receive a rich gift today insures the reception of a richer gift tomorrow (p.148).

"Do you think I am less delighted to give My gifts to you than you are to share peach ice cream with your friends?" God's voice asked. "Do you think I want you to hesitate to ask for more?"

In excitement I burst into my husband's study, astonishing him by exclaiming, "He wants us to ask for more! He wants to give us more!" And God does have that great desire. Our not asking is the only thing that holds Him back from pouring out more of heaven's blessing upon us.

Not all of God's training is discipline. It is true that we seem to learn best by correction and discipline. But how much He longs for children eager to listen to His voice as He imparts the wisdom of the ages to us in quietness and peace. He wants us to have a keen longing to know Him better. How much better to have listened to the voice of Jesus and gained understanding during the quietness of our prayer times with Him than to have to acquire the same lesson through trial and tribulation.

Many, many have been the lessons God has taught me under trial. But now and then I reach out and grasp one of His gifts during the stillness of communion with Him.

One night as I prepared for bed I felt that I had totally wasted my day. Deeply repentant, I asked the Lord to forgive me. While I knew He was always willing to forgive, I sorrowed that I had learned nothing of Him that day. Picking up my Bible, I asked Him to reveal Himself to me in a special way through His Word.

My Bible fell open to Matthew 17:20. "For truly, I say unto you, if you have faith as a grain of mustard seed, you will say to this mountain, 'Move from here to there,' and it will move; and nothing will be impossible to you" (RSV).

"O Lord," I said in disappointment, "I already understand that verse. It means that faith is so powerful that, like the atom bomb, a very tiny bit of faith can work miracles."

I can almost imagine that God smiled as He answered me.

"My dear Carrol, you're wrong. In fact, just the opposite is true. Because there is *no power* in faith, even a very little bit of faith is ample to produce miracles. You see, the power is not in faith, but wholly in *Me!* A mustard seed of faith is all that is necessary. All you need is that faith that reaches up and connects with *Me.*"

At that the Holy Spirit illumined my mind, and I suddenly understood. All we need to do is to cry out to God, "Lord, I believe, help thou my unbelief!" Even that sort of weak faith produces miracles because it is not our faith but our God that is powerful! The only sort of extraordinary faith that is available is that same mustard seed of faith being constantly exercised. No one need protest lack of faith as an excuse for lack of miracles in his life. God gives everyone a portion of faith, and the slightest fragment of that unused, rusty, and dusty faith will produce miracles, not because of its inherent power, but because of God's wonderful love and unending power.

However, there is a beautiful difference between Great Faith and Little Faith. Little Faith searches frantically here and there for answers to life's problems and finally in desperation turns to God for the solution. When Great Faith meets a problem it immediately turns to God as naturally as a flower turns to the sun.

How gracious of God to answer my prayer for wisdom at the end of that wasted day. God delights to give gifts to the unworthy. He bestowed His Son on our unworthy world. O Lord, I'm asking for more!

One day my husband and I drove toward the mountains for a brief respite from the city heat. We had a picnic supper stowed away in a basket and the luxury of two hours to squander. As we rode along we discussed the relationship of faith and obedience. Such a basic Christian principle to cause such furor around the world!

I had read in a book that faith is like a door. When you open the door of faith the other side of that same door bears the marking "Obedience." I liked that.

We had been studying the book of John in our small group for just a short while and were filled with the concepts of Jesus who came to reveal God. Now on that trip to the mountains God presented me with a new illustration for faith and obedience.

Obedience makes faith visible just as Jesus made God visible. In the same way that God had to reveal Himself in a human body to be perceived by human eyes, so must our faith be put into tangible actions before it is visible to others. Actually, without the actions of faith there is no faith at all.

The book of James became real as God shared with us the basis for the apostle's declaration that "I will show you my faith by what I do" (James 2:18). Jesus came to disclose what otherwise could never be seen. As God is invisible to human eyes without Jesus, so faith cannot be perceived without human actions.

Sometimes God's instructions may come at a time when you do not even realize you are in a contemplative frame of mind. Once I drove into the parking lot of the Faculty Medical Offices for a doctor's appointment. It was a beautiful sunny day, and I reveled in the songs of the birds, the green grass, the bright flowers. As I got out of the car I noticed a gardener on a lawn mower. God called my attention to him in an impressive way that is hard to put into words. The man was some distance away: I could not distinguish his features. But it was as though God said to me, "Do you see that man? He is My precious child, and just as important to Me as the influential doctors here at Loma Linda. The man is not important to me *in spite of* his lack of polish and education and the work he does, but rather *because* of all this. In My plan he is just as necessary, just as dear, as the president of Loma Linda University. You should regard him as someone to be desired as a friend or church member. And you should take a special interest in such men and women."

How can you help but love and worship a God like that? No outward pomp impresses our God, only a willing, teachable heart.

Summary

G od is always seeking to reveal more of Himself to us. He is eager to find a hungering, empty heart that He can fill.

We seem to learn most of our lessons through the anguish of trial and discipline. Yet God longs for us to so hunger and thirst after righteousness that He can give us His choicest gifts in our quiet times of communion with Him.

How delighted He is when we come to Him in *expectation* of a blessing. He will never turn us away unfilled.

12

The Sound
of His Voice

A lthough God often speaks to us in His still small voice through our minds, yet sometimes he uses other human voices to present His words. I have already related how God has used other Christians, either in person or through books, to break through thought barriers in my mind and allow me to see a new view of God. Sometimes, though, God uses even childish voices.

Several years ago, while we still lived in the interim house between the big house we built and the place we are residing in now, my two little granddaughters spent an afternoon with me. As I worked in the kitchen 6-year-old Tami asked me how it was that I never yelled or got mad. It pleased me that I had been able to be a good witness to the girls, and I was just opening my mouth to say that when Jesus is in your heart you don't yell or get mad, or some such pious remark, when 4-year-old Kimi shattered my self-righteousness.

"Well, Grandma," she said, "I've heard you whine around sometimes."

Outward anger and yelling are not my failings. Complaining is. My 4-year-old granddaughter had seen to the heart of the matter.

Not long afterward we moved to our present house. As usual, the move came at an inconvenient time. We were just completing a Revelation Seminar. Having hurt my back in the move, I definitely did not feel my best. The evangelist holding the Revelation Seminar announced that the final class would be on Sabbath morning with a special dinner following for all the guests, furnished by the church ladies. Immediately I planned what I would bring, an ample amount, but then I began to be concerned as I heard little comment about the potluck from anyone else. I feared that the whole meal would be a disaster with hundreds showing up and not even enough food for a dozen. My worry began to take over my prayer time. I could not keep my mind on my devotions.

"Lord," I finally prayed, "you know I'm taking all the food I can for this dinner. I can't furnish the whole meal! What's going to happen? I hate to have our whole Revelation Seminar discredited because we advertise a free meal and then don't come through on it."

As usual the Lord set me in my place.

"Are you in charge of the food?" He asked me.

The thought took me aback. No one had asked me to take command of the food. It was my self-appointed task, and that only in my mind. Clearly the Lord showed me that if I have accepted the responsibility of overseeing something, then I must carefully plan it. And if I am not in charge, I should do my part but leave the arrangements to the proper people. Often since that time, when my Martha mind begins its familiar track, God reminds me, "Are you in charge of the food?"

Sabbath came with our final Revelation Seminar followed by a delicious vegetarian meal for our many guests. Did we have enough food, you ask? Oh, yes, it was a fantastic display of salads, vegetables, entreés, breads, and desserts, with plenty for seconds for everyone. They didn't need me to take charge of the food.

Not long afterward I reread the little book *Hind's Feet on High Places,* by Hannah Hurnard. In the story, an allegory, the heroine is little crippled Much-Afraid, who typifies each of us on our heavenward journey. The Shepherd promises Much-Afraid a new name when she has learned to walk on the heights with Him. First she receives hind's feet to replace her crippled ones and then a new name, Grace and Glory.

The book really touches my heart, for I can identify so well with Much-Afraid. I live her encounters with her deadly cousins, Pride, Self-Pity, Resentment, and Craven Fear.

When I finished the book God gently told me that my name had been Worry and Complaining for a long time. But He had chosen a new name for me, Trusting and Rejoicing. With His strength I can walk with hind's feet on high places and become forever-after Trusting and Rejoicing.

One more story reveals the lavishness of God's forgiveness.

It was nearly Christmas right after we had moved into our present house. We had just finished the Revelation Seminar, Thanksgiving rushed past, and I was still suffering with a bad back and a cold. Naturally it seemed to me that it was going to be impossible to be ready for Christmas that year. I finally managed to collect, wrap, and mail the packages for family out of town. Time was so short that I had only one day clear in my schedule to shop for gifts for my husband, my oldest son who lived nearby, and my daughter, her husband, and my two granddaughters. I love the holiday when I have time to sew and bake, and shop leisurely. But I hate shopping in the crowded stores just before Christmas and seldom even attempt it. But this year it seemed necessary if anybody was to receive any gifts from Mom and Dad.

It was a cloudy morning as I backed out of our driveway for my shopping spree. I decided to begin at the big discount store where prices were the lowest. Quickly I made my selections, piled them in a basket, and joined a block-long line to pay for them. An hour later I emerged to find the rain pouring down. By the time I got my things in the car, I wanted to do nothing so much as to go home. But it was my only day for shopping. I drove through the rain to a shopping mall and dashed into the first department store. (I had left my umbrella at home, of course!) There I chose robes and slippers for my two granddaughters, plus little overalls for a baby shower gift, and again waited in a long line. When it came my turn I had my checkbook out and the date and my signature already on the check. Since we had just moved, my new checks had not yet arrived and I was still using the old ones. To facilitate matters, I had crossed out the old address and written in the new one by hand. The telephone number was the same. The clerk took one look at my check and said, "I can't take this. Since you've written on it, it's the same as a blank check. We aren't allowed to take blank checks." I stared at her in astonishment. Surely she didn't really mean she wasn't going to let me buy the things I had chosen. But she did. "Well, just keep your things then," I exclaimed, thrusting the clothes across the counter and stomping angrily out of the store.

Once outside I stopped in dismay. More than dismay—in horror. Could that have really been *me* who became angry? In abject humiliation I bowed my head. "O Lord," I prayed, "please forgive me for disgracing Your name."

I wanted so badly to give up, to just go home, but I had to finish my shopping. It was my only day. So I walked dejectedly down the mall to the department store at the farthest end and went to the children's department. Again I selected robes and slippers and little overalls. A clerk asked if she could help me. I explained my predicament, and she went to check with her department head. Yes, they'd take my check. Completing my purchases, I walked slowly back down the mall. The thing to do, I decided, was to make no notation on my check at all. Just let them think I still lived there. It worked at the next shop, where I purchased my husband's gift.

Leaving the mall, I started homeward. Two more stops and then I could call an end to the whole horrible day. Again I hunted and finally found a parking place in a crowded lot, then made a dash through the rain for the store. As quickly as I could, I made my selections and once more stood in a long line. I had my check ready with no changes on it. The clerk took it, looked it over, and asked, "Is all the information on this check correct?" My heart began beating faster. If I said no, she wouldn't let me buy my things. How could I bear to lie? I mumbled, "Um." The woman obviously considered I was hard of hearing and raised her voice. "Is all the information on this check correct?" she loudly demanded.

"Yes," I muttered.

Sadly I picked up my packages and sought my car. I didn't even notice the rain as I unlocked the door. What kind of Christian was I that here in one day I had become angry and now I had lied? It left me sick in my heart. "Oh, my Father," I humbly pleaded, "all I can say is please forgive me."

The tears in my eyes almost equaled the downpour of the rain as I once again turned my car into the street toward home. One more stop.

Here I had enough cash to pay for the purchase. The line was short and I was soon finished. I pushed the door open and stood transfixed. Across the sky God had flung a rainbow. Its hues were of a brilliance I have never seen before or since.

Rapturous joy replaced the sorrow in my heart. "Thank You, thank You, Father. I know now that no matter how great my sin You freely forgive me!" All the way home I gazed at that rainbow. All the way home I rejoiced in a lavish, loving, forgiving God.

Of course, you may say that God didn't send that rainbow just for me. You're right. I'm sure He had other purposes for it as well. But let me tell you that none was more important than the comfort He brought me that terrible, beautiful day.

> The heavens declare the glory of God;
>> the skies proclaim the work of his hands.
> Day after day they pour forth speech;
>> night after night they display knowledge.
> There is no speech or language
>> where their voice is not heard.
> Their voice goes out into all the earth,
>> their words to the ends of the world (Psalm 19:1-4).

The voice of God has many timbres. Only the heart attuned to hear His voice can be sure to recognize the variety and the lavishness of the ways He chooses to speak to His human children.

Summary

The Lord speaks to us in many different voices:

1. Through a still small voice in our minds.
2. Through fellow Christians.
3. Through the little ones—our children, or others' children.
4. Through books.
5. Through nature.

We must learn to recognize His voice and respond.

13

Altars
Along the Way

All along the way I have found it beneficial to set up roadmarks—or altars, if you please—to remind me of special times in my relationship with Jesus. You see, I have found that it helps to have something to look at and remember when Satan thrusts his insinuations at me. Otherwise, I might believe him.

The early patriarchs erected altars under God's direction, not only to worship Him at that particular time, but also to *remind* them later of a special experience with their Lord. Whenever anyone, even a pagan, came upon an altar to the true God, he could have his thoughts directed heavenward. The altar was a reminder to all of the everlasting God.

Now, my altars were not visible and can be seen by others only as I put them into words. However, they are clearly marked in my mind. Every story I have related in this book is one of my cherished altars. Many of my most used roadmarks are Scripture verses that I have discovered (really been shown to me by God, of course!) at the exact time I needed them. Indelibly impressed upon my heart, they are always ready to be brought to my attention when Satan buffets me with his discouragements. When the devil tells me that I might as well give up, that I'm hopelessly weak, and that God just can't save me, this "altar" comes into mind:

> Being confident of this, that he who began
> a good work in you will carry in on to
> completion until the day of Christ Jesus (Philippians 1:6).

As I remember this great promise that God gave me to break a deep spiritual depression in my past, it brings to mind another altar, too, the time of my conversion. Thus, just as Abraham left behind him a series of altars as he traveled to Canaan, so in my life one altar leads to another.

Brought up in a Seventh-day Adventist home, I had always loved the Lord in my careless, frivolous youthful way. I was quick in mind, quick in motion, quick to laugh, quick to cry. Nothing penetrated much below the surface.

When I became a teenager I began to evaluate what being a Christian would mean to my life, and it seemed that I would miss out on too much. Thus I did not choose to be a Christian, deciding instead that I would wait until after I had tried the world.

When I was 13 my two sisters, ages 14 and 9, began taking baptismal classes at school. Because of sickness I did not attend school that year, and so I was not involved in the classes. When the pastor planned my sisters' baptism, Mother included my name on the list. She had no way of knowing that I had decided not to be baptized and that I was too softhearted to tell her. Instead I brought up every health-related excuse I could think of, all to no avail. The minister assured me that the Lord would protect my health and no harm would come to me from the baptismal water. And so a day came that should have been a momentous occasion for me. Instead I was filled with uneasiness.

My sisters and I were baptized in the beautiful outdoor setting of a river. I remember walking out into the water with the pastor, but there my memory ends. The event carried no spiritual significance whatsoever, unless it separated me further from God, for now I was a hypocrite.

Over the years I often tried to be a Christian for short periods of time. I really did love God and I surely wanted to be saved in heaven. Besides that, I longed to be a good person. But Christianity asked too much. There was so much I yearned to find out about life.

Finally I grew disgusted with attempting both to be a Christian and to enjoy the world. So I made my decision. I would leave the church and end the hypocrisy. Going to my mother, I told her what I had decided, suspecting that she would ask me to leave home. My older sister had already done so, and Mother often wept at night because of some of the older girl's choices. Still I felt I had to be honest with Mother this time, even if it hurt her.

When I presented my decision to her, she asked me what I planned to do in the immediate future. As I didn't really have that thought out, she wisely suggested that I remain at home and attend college until I had made some concrete plans. She said that of course she would expect me to live by Christian standards as long as I stayed there. I suspect that I felt secretly relieved, really not ready to move out on my own. Instead I enrolled in college again that fall and life went on for me much the way it had for several years. Except that now I had taken my stand against Christianity and my barriers were down.

The greatest attraction in the world for me at that time was movies. I just couldn't seem to get enough of them. One Sunday a girlfriend and I had gone to the nearby city and watched three double features—six movies in all. (Of course, it went against the standards Mother had requested me to obey. But my heart was not obedient to any rules—home, school, or church.)

We had missed the last bus home and had to walk several miles in the rain. As we did so I realized that I was coming down with a cold. My throat ached and I was tired all over. Surely I would miss school tomorrow and perhaps even all week. I could find only one thing good about it.

"The fall Week of Prayer begins tomorrow," I said to my girlfriend. "At least now I won't have to sit in chapel and listen to a speaker begging me to forsake my sins," I giggled miserably.

I was right. I was very sick. The only bright spot that miserable Monday was the realization that I would most likely escape the entire Week of Prayer. That was something. At least I'd picked the right week to be sick. All day long I lay in bed dozing, then waking, glad that I was not sitting through the meetings.

Mother came home from work late in the afternoon. She tried to ease my misery with a glass of cold juice, then handed me a letter.

"This was in the mail for you," she said as she left the room to fix dinner.

A spark of interest poked through my wretchedness. Eagerly I ripped open the envelope and unfolded the pages.

"Dearest Chum," the letter began. It was from one of my closest friends who had married a young ministerial student the year before. Because Bernice no longer ran around with our crowd, I had not told her of my decision to leave off hypocrisy and join the world. Now she wrote of her concern as she had heard of some of my activities.

"Carrol," Bernice said, "my husband and I and some of our friends are praying especially for you this Week of Prayer. It is our desire that you realize the important place God should have in your life."

"This is none of your business," I retorted angrily. "You have no right to write to me like this!" I turned over and began pounding my pillow. Wasn't it enough that Mother was praying for me and weeping over my behavior? Did Bernice have to gather a *crowd* to pray for me? Wasn't it my own personal business if I wanted to be a Christian or not? The anger and the tears flowed out together. Suddenly I was tired of fighting.

"O God," I prayed, "What am I to do?"

"Stop fighting Me." The answer flooded into my mind. "It's so easy to surrender. And in that surrender you'll find your heart's desire."

To this day I cannot explain my conversion in a logical way. I wanted nothing to do with God. I was angry when a friend even mentioned my relationship with God. Yet the frustrated tears of that 19-year-old girl became ones of repentance in less than a moment of time. The loving Jesus had broken down my resistance and given me the real desire of my heart.

It was real, too. I changed completely, never to go back to the old independent thinking. Of course I don't mean that I became perfect overnight. You've read my story and you know better than that. But since that time I have never desired to go back to the world. While I have often wallowed in selfish sins and made myself miserable, yet I have always known that my heart really longed only for Jesus.

I didn't become a mature Christian immediately. But I did begin a wholehearted love affair with Jesus. In my typical fashion I composed poetry, chattered to all my friends about Him, wrote letters about His charms. A typical adolescent in love, I never dreamed that I would ever be restless again or need anything to make me happy save His presence.

By Friday of that Week of Prayer I returned to school. Longing to have a real baptism now that I loved Jesus, I made an appointment with the visiting speaker who had conducted the meetings. But I was too shy with adults to be able to express my needs to someone who was a total stranger to me. He told me that since I had been baptized, I could not do it again. Sadly I turned away.

I married my young minister just a little more than a year later. Whenever I heard an evangelist preach on baptism I felt a heart cry to be really baptized. When I discussed it with my husband he was sympathetic, though startled. For who had ever heard of a minister's wife needing to be baptized? What would people think? So I buried my desire for a true baptism and went on growing in Jesus.

The years passed by and I learned more and more about my God. At the same time I found many people who also had been baptized during their unthinking youth. They had been baptized in our schools, maybe with the entire eighth-grade class, or perhaps as a result of parental or pastoral persuasion. I saw many of them now being rebaptized as a part of their *real* new birth. My longing for a true baptism resurfaced.

Yet I realized that my experience differed from theirs.

They were only now *beginning* their walk with Jesus but I had been journeying with Him for many years. I longed to be baptized, and yet I realized that people would wonder what terrible sin the minister's wife had fallen into that she had to be rebaptized. Even if I gave my testimony in church the day I was baptized, there would be many who would not understand. Desiring only to glorify God, not dishonor His name in any way, I asked the Lord if He wanted me to be publicly baptized—but could not feel that He was saying yes. Why then did I have this longing for a meaningful baptism?

One Thursday afternoon I sat down for a moment to read my Bible and began in Romans 6.

> What shall we say, then? Shall we go on sinning
> so that grace may increase? By no means! We died
> to sin; how can we live in it any longer? Or don't
> you know that all of us who were baptized into Christ
> Jesus were baptized into his death? We were there-
> fore buried with him through baptism into death
> in order that, just as Christ was raised from the
> dead through the glory of the Father, we too may
> live a new life (verses 1-4).

As I read, my heart cried out to make those promises mine.

"O Lord," I responded to the tugging at my heart, "how I envy those who can remember the sincerity of their baptismal vows. I wish I could claim these very verses for my life."

Before going out for the evening I decided to take a shower. Such occasions were often good times to discuss things with my Lord. As I prepared for the shower my yearning for the blessings of baptism continued. Then the Lord startled me with His comment.

"You don't need another public display of baptism for

others to see a change in your life because you have long belonged to Me. By the water in this shower I symbolize the cleansing of My blood that I have already begun in your life. You are clean. All those promises are yours."

As the water poured over me I rejoiced and praised God. I truly felt new all over.

Immediately dressing, I hurried with my husband to a wedding rehearsal and then to a rehearsal dinner. The next morning we had an extremely important and traumatic appointment and then the wedding in the afternoon. After the wedding we rushed home and got our things in the car and hurried off to a mountain weekend retreat for our church. "Hurry" seemed to be our middle name.

The hectic rush wiped the memory of the incident from my mind. I did not even tell my husband. Saturday night a group of us sat around the campfire. One girl began telling of the work Jesus was doing in her life and of His intervention by means of a powerful dream. As I listened I felt God's nudge.

"Tell them about your baptism," He said. And the wonderful memory flooded my mind.

Altars are an aid to worship. Old Testament altars usually consisted of stone. My altars are made only of memories, memories of victories in Jesus. Every day I am building new altars, new victories.

Summary

We all need reminders of the special blessings God has given us. It would be well if we reviewed often each answered prayer, each time when the presence of God seemed especially near, each Bible verse the Holy Spirit has highlighted in our minds, each time the Lord has been noticeably merciful.

To facilitate such remembering, I suggest keeping a spiritual notebook that you can often reread. Personally I use a 5″ x 7″ loose-leaf notebook, keeping it near my special place of morning prayer so that it is easy to pick up either to reread or to make an entry. I keep my entries simple, and I don't try to make them literary masterpieces. Dating the top of the page, I then briefly list any special insights God has given me or narrate a short story of God's leading or blessing. Sometimes it may be a Bible verse or verses that God has given me new meaning for. Other times I may feel impressed to put my words into a prayer or poem of praise or experience. I do not make an entry every day, but only when I feel a special need to remember something.

14

Cherished Sin and Prayer

What is a cherished sin, anyway? I've always figured that it must be pretty attractive. Aren't the things that we cherish in our homes usually quite nice? That lovely picture painted by a friend, that little figurine we've had for years, that bowl just the perfect shape for holding so many things? We don't cherish *ugly* things. Or do we?

Not too long ago the Lord showed me that any sinful tendency that I have not overcome is a cherished sin. I may *hate* it, but if it has control over me in any way, it is a cherished sin, for I have not yet yielded it to the Lord.

I think the devil succeeds well in fooling us about this. When we *hate* some characteristic in ourselves and have often prayed about it, we do not see it as something we cling to. After all, are we not seeking to be rid of it instead of trying to hang on to it?

It is easy for me to see novel reading and daydreaming as something treasured, for I *enjoy* them so much. But it is much harder for me to recognize a spirit of judging and my critical nature (jealousy, self-pity, complaining, resentment) as things that I am reluctant to give up, for I *hate* them as much as I enjoy the others. They make me so miserable that surely I am not clinging to them. Yet God tells us that sin shall not have dominion over us if we walk in His Spirit (Romans 8). So evidently as long as such sins remain evident in my life, I am *cherishing* them.

We always face danger when we allow any sin, whether inherited or cultivated, to linger in our lives. It will not stay dormant indefinitely, but will eventually grow and control us. Meanwhile it may hide truth, muffle the voice of Jesus, and lead us in wrong paths.

The role of Jesus in the Most Holy Place, His work of investigation, is to bring out of hiding all such sins so that we can see them for what they are and repent and put them away. Thus God will have a people cleansed of sin to receive the Holy Spirit in fullness.

God has illustrated to me in my own life the dangers of cherished sin. Because this story involves others besides myself I cannot share any details but I can pass on the dramatic lesson God taught me.

God's transformations in my life often involve the relationships among our family members. One specific problem seemed insurmountable to me. I listened to one person and then to another. What could be truth? Where was God leading? No approach seemed right to me. I had no way to know and yet my decision was important to all. Thus I spent hours wrestling in prayer over the problem. But as I concluded one prayer session I had a frightening experience that I knew did not come from God. Numbed, I arose from my knees and staggered through a weary day. "If the devil can enter my prayer time with Jesus, what safety have I?" I questioned God. "How can I ever know truth? Is it never possible to be perfectly protected from the evil one?"

Our just God has nothing to hide and everything to reveal. Always open with us, He delights to have us come to him with honest questions. God revealed to me that day that a cherished sin of mine touched upon the problem I was seeking an answer for. This sin which I did not have victory over—one that I hated, by the way—left me unprotected from Satan in that area. Because I had cherished a self-righteous attitude toward a member of my family, Satan could confuse my prayer time. Two Bible verses came to mind.

> Satan himself masquerades as an angel of light (2 Corinthians 11:14).

> For false Christs and false prophets will appear
> and perform great signs and miracles to deceive
> even the elect—if that were possible (Matthew 24:24).

I could see that although we think of both verses in connection with the time when Satan will impersonate Christ and deceive nearly all the world, they have another meaning also. The devil will be able to come as an angel of light to any who have cherished sins in their lives. *Satan himself will answer their prayers.*

The Lord helped me to see the many times that the same spirit of self-righteousness had touched not only my relationship with this person but also all in the circle of my influence. The memory of the experience still leaves me humbled and submissive.

Any sin that repeatedly crops up in my life is a danger signal. Sometimes we learn to tolerate the sin simply because of its recurrences. Or we avoid conflict that might expose it. But God, because He loves us so much, and because time is short, must expose our sins. He reveals them first to us. If we repent and forsake them, He blots them out. But if we refuse to acknowledge the sin, He will bring it to light before others (see Proverbs 26:26 and Proverbs 28:13).

> When we are judged by the Lord, we are
> being disciplined so that we will not be condemned
> with the world (1 Corinthians 11:32).

When I began seriously cooperating with God in His mission of investigation in my life, I eagerly awaited each new disclosure. Not until then did I realize the extent of sin in my life. Or the trauma it would cause as I faced major changes. Many of the lessons I learned about myself came through hard trials.

Of course, the lovely thing about God's discipline is that it always has a spirit of expectancy about it—even when it's hurting. The buoyancy and joy of the Holy Spirit holds you up even though the waves of trouble swirl all around you.

One thing to remember about sin of all types—if your eyes focus upon the sin, you cannot see Jesus. The *only* way to eliminate it is to allow Jesus to cleanse you.

> If we confess our sins, he is faithful and
> just to forgive us our sins, and to cleanse
> us from all unrighteousness (1 John 1:9, KJV).

THE HEART CLEANING

> I had read it often
> in poem and prose—
> my heart must be clean
> to let Christ in.
> He only stays where
> purity and peace abide.

But as I cleaned,
preparatory to asking
Him in to stay,
the dirt and drivel
poured over my doorstep
like a tidal wave
until my heart
was buried in the deluge.

"O God," I cried,
as I shoveled away,
"what shall I do?"

"Just ask Me in,"
He whispered above
the clamorous noise
of jostling sins.

And so, in shame, I did.
And in a minute
He'd swept my heart bare.
Like a nerve uncovered,
I felt His power
as He closed the door with
Him inside.

Together we furnished
my heart in
godly fashion and
He switched on heavenly music
and eternal light.
That's the way
it's been ever since.

Don't tell me that you
want to clean and fancy
your heart for Him.
It can't be done.
There's only one way—
    Just ask Him in.

Summary

A ny sinful tendency that has control of my life is a cherished sin, even if I hate it. We often think of cherished sin as self-indulgence in pleasure only, such as:

1. Overeating.
2. Drinking alcoholic beverages.
3. Promiscuous sex.
4. Laziness.
5. Wrong TV watching, etc.

But we must also include the things we hate:

1. Jealousy.
2. Self-pity.
3. Complaining.
4. Anger.
5. Resentment, impatience, etc.

God's final sanctuary ministry has as its goal to bring out of hiding our cherished sins and reveal them to us so that we can repent and be cleansed.

15

Survivors; Dwellers in the Most Holy Place

Earth time is fast running out. The story line of the Bible has almost reached its end. While the events of the book of Revelation unfold—earthquakes, wars, pestilences, famine, and fire—the parable of the ten virgins steadily approaches its conclusion within the church of God. Sad to say, most of the actors do not realize the importance of the parts they are playing.

At the time when God began revealing to me what He desired to do for me in the Most Holy Place, Isaiah 4:2-6 shone out bright and clear as God's plan for my life.

> In that day the Branch of the Lord will be beautiful and glorious, and the fruit of the land will be the pride and glory of the survivors in Israel. Those who are left in Zion, who remain in Jerusalem, will be called holy, all who are recorded among the living in Jerusalem. The Lord will wash away the filth of the women of Zion; he will cleanse the bloodstains from Jerusalem by a spirit of judgment and a spirit of fire. Then the Lord will create over all of Mount Zion and over those who assemble there a cloud of smoke by day

and a glow of flaming fire by night; over all
the glory will be a canopy. It will be a shelter
and shade from the heat of the day, and a refuge
and hiding place from the storm and rain.

The last phase of Christ's mediatorial work for our small rebellious planet is nearing completion. The three angels are shouting out their last warnings to a dying world. It is not something that is going to happen way off in the future. Rather, it concerns *my* life and *my* time. The warnings about getting ready for the last days are for me, now. This is serious, soul-searching business, and it must be my major concern. I can't put it off until a convenient time. The work of making me ready to live with Jesus for eternity must be done now if it is ever done at all.

"For out of Jerusalem will come a remnant,
And out of Mount Zion a *band of survivors.*
The zeal of the Lord Almighty
will accomplish this" (Isaiah 37:32).

Perfection is not something you put on like a garment in a moment of time. As you accept the free gift of the robe of Christ's righteousness and thus become blameless in the sight of God, the Holy Spirit begins to work inward to purify your life itself. Cooperation with the discipline of God is the only way such cleansing can work, as God has planned no salvation without the total consent and participation of the human being. It is the only way He can have a perfectly free and sinless universe for eternity. God knows our needs. He has written special advice for our very day:

"To the angel of the church in Laodicea write:
"These are the words of the Amen, the
faithful and true witness, the ruler of God's
creation. I know your deeds, that you are

neither cold nor hot. . . . I am about to spit you out
of my mouth. You say, 'I am rich; I have
acquired wealth and do not need a thing.' But
you do not realize that you are wretched,
pitiful, poor, blind and naked. I counsel you
to buy from me gold refined in the fire, so you
can become rich; and white clothes to wear, so
you can cover your shameful nakedness; and salve
to put on your eyes, so you can see.

"Those whom I love I rebuke and discipline.
So be earnest, and repent. Here I am! I stand
at the door and knock. If anyone hears my voice
and opens the door, I will come in and eat with
him, and he with me.

"To him who overcomes, I will give the right
to sit with me on my throne, just as I overcame
and sat down with my Father on his throne.
He who has an ear, let him hear what the Spirit
says to the churches" (Revelation 3:14-22).

O Lord, give us ears to hear Your special messages to
us today! The final events of human history are upon us.
Revelation 14:1-5 describes the band of survivors who will
greet Jesus upon His triumphant return to put an end to
sin. Becoming a survivor is the sole life task of each of us.
But being a survivor is not a solitary thing. Although we
are saved individually, yet each has a part in the work of
rescuing many others. Earthly survival often means tram-
pling upon others to save yourself. But heavenly survival
is saving yourself by helping others.

In 1844, at the close of the 2300-day prophecy
mentioned in Daniel 7, Jesus entered the Most Holy Place
to begin the task of winding up the last events here on
earth. There He judges and cleanses a people who will be
safe to mingle in a sinless universe for all eternity. It is a
work done in each human heart, as well as in heaven.

When I began "sanctuary praying," using the pattern of

the earthly sanctuary as a form for my daily prayer (described in chapter six), God began revealing to me the plague spots in my character. But sometimes I had difficulty in being honest enough to allow the Lord to probe into their depths. And in order for Him to do that, He must have my total cooperation. He will never use force. So sometimes the Lord just had to let time elapse before I was again willing to continue.

Another problem was my constant conviction that surely He had reached the end of my sin and now all would be rosy and happy. The Lord had to continually say, "There's more, Carrol, much more." I had to learn to find my enjoyment in the *process* of sanctification, rather than expecting to have it *accomplished* quickly.

Recently I have discovered another aid to help me in cooperating with God in Most Holy Place praying. It is a special type of prayer, one that concentrates on the cleansing of the mind and memories to rid the heart of all sin, resentments, and animosities. A friend who was finding great blessing in his life from using it first suggested it to me. I have adapted his prayer into a 10-part Most Holy Place prayer that has been a continual blessing not only to myself, but to my husband and to others to whom we seek to minister. The 10 steps of the prayer of cleansing are:

1. Pray to commit your life to God. ("Lord, I'm wholly Yours. Make me willing to listen to Your voice. Make me receptive.")

2. Pray for heavenly protection. (The devil is real. Ask for a canopy of angels to surround you.)

3. Ask God what weakness or sin in your life He wants to reveal to you today. (Wait for His response.)

4. Ask God how this has affected you all your life. (Wait for the answer.)

5. Pray, "Lord, take me back in my life to the very first moment this sin entered my life. Show me how it began, the experience, the people involved." (Wait for the answer.)

6. Now make the choice to freely give the sin to Jesus.

Example of a prayer of giving up the sin:

"Dear Father: I give You my sin; take it from me. I do not want it. I see how it has affected me all my life, and I want to give it up. I freely choose You to control my mind and body."

7. Pray, "In place of this sin, Lord, show me what attribute of Christ's character You want to give me." (Wait for the answer.)

8. Pray, "Lord Jesus, thank You for the healing You have just given me. I ask You to weave it through all of my life to the present moment."

You may repeat steps 3 through 8 for as long as you feel the Lord is leading you to continue. But always be sure you conclude with steps 9 and 10.

9. Pray, "Lord Jesus, I long to see the cross of Calvary. Take me in mind to the cross and show me what You want me to view today. Show me Jesus and His special message for me." (Wait for the answer.)

10. Finally, pray, "Now, Lord, I ask for a special infilling of the Holy Spirit throughout all my body. Fill my feet and my hands that I may willingly be of service to You. Fill my heart, Lord, that only You can ever possess it. Fill my eyes, my ears, my mouth, my lips, my brain, my mind, my emotions. Fill all of me that I may belong to You only, forever and eternally."

The steps of prayer I have given here are only samples to help you in understanding what is involved. The Lord will give you your own. This cleansing prayer may be used effectively in a group with one person leading and the rest repeating it phrase by phrase.

Perhaps before I go any further I should state some cautions. As I have mentioned before, I do not believe anyone has to recite a certain prayer in order to be saved. No form of prayer has any specific saving power. Not only that, no impression, either during prayer or at any other time, comes with an automatic divine insignia that declares it to be the voice of God. Any such impression must be first relevant to God's will and then tested by the word of God (1 John 4:1). Furthermore, do not let this type of introspective prayer take the time and place of daily Bible study. It is only by personal application of the Word of God that this prayer can really be effective.

Time is short and the transformation must be done quickly. I believe the Lord is showing us how to speed up the changes in our lives and in the lives of those around us. Our children must mature quickly in Christian character. And how can we help others if we are not conscious of our own defects? Let me share with you how the Lord has worked through such praying in my life:

The other morning when I got to the Most Holy Place in my prayer time I asked Jesus what He wanted to show me that day about my life. The word that appeared in my mind was *anger*. Now, I was sure that was not my problem, so I argued with God.

"You know I'm not angry, Lord. There must be some mistake." Often I immediately recognize the problem in my life, but this time I couldn't see it.

"You're not *outwardly* angry now," He replied, "but

look back in your life. Do you recognize any anger?" In amazement I saw and felt again the strength of my feelings toward my older sister when I thought of throwing her through the plate-glass living room window. I remembered the horror of an even younger me who had thrown a flashlight battery at the same sister and cut her arm —barely missing her temple, in which case I could have badly injured her. Yes, I had to admit, there was anger.

"Look back even further," God advised me. Then I saw in my mind a 2-year-old girl crying on the front porch as she watched her mother and older sister walking off to Sabbath school while she had to stay home with Daddy.

"I wasn't angry," I said. "I was only hurt because I couldn't go to Sabbath school too."

"What happened next?" the Lord asked. Memory flooded in. The little girl had lost control, and the results were typical of a 2-year-old.

"Yes, Lord, take away the anger that has polluted my life and heal me," I prayed.

Of course, this work in our lives does not depend upon praying my special prayer. Often the Lord shows me similar things in totally unprayerlike circumstances.

One Sunday morning my husband and I attended the wedding of one of our church members. We took seats on the groom's side, just behind the relatives' section. Right ahead of us sat the wife of one of the groom's brothers, small and all alone with no part in the wedding celebration. The Lord immediately nudged me and reminded me of another wedding, that of my husband's sister. My husband had been the officiating minister, my younger sister the maid of honor, and I had sat all alone with no part in the celebration. I guess I really hadn't been alone, though, for Resentment and Self-pity occupied the pew with me. The Lord reminded me that this was typical of me in any situation in which I was not either the center of attention or at least directly involved.

"O Lord," I immediately prayed, "change me. Forgive me and heal me of my many self-centered years. I want to be different. Make me, Lord, like Jesus."

Let me emphasize that such an examination of my life is to be conducted only by Jesus through the Holy Spirit. It is not my own work, and the end result is never to make me feel guilty. Rather its goal is *repentance*. Repentance always produces forgiveness, and forgiveness brings salvation. Never, never get caught up in any type of self-examination of your *emotions* that preoccupies your mind and makes you useless for service. *Jesus* must always be the object of our thoughts and His service supreme. Our commission at this time is to seek to cooperate fully with our High Priest as He concludes the Most Holy Place ministry of the heavenly sanctuary. If we learn to listen carefully to His voice and follow His directions, He will be enabled to make an end of sin in our lives.

Life is changing fast around us. Our earthly supports are disappearing. "As it was in the days of Noah, so it will be at the coming of the Son of Man. . . . So you also must be ready, because the Son of Man will come at an hour when you do not expect him" (Matthew 24:37-44).

I want to be a survivor. I know that is your wish too. What a glorious opportunity is ours, to be a part of God's final display of grace.

> "The ransomed of the Lord will return.
> They will enter Zion with singing;
> everlasting joy will crown their heads.
> Gladness and joy will overtake them,
> and sorrow and sighing will flee away" (Isaiah 51:11).

Summary

The ministry of Jesus in the Most Holy Place is nearing completion. Without our cooperation the final work for us individually cannot be done. How God longs for an intelligent response and cooperation on the part of His people! We need to be willing to accept His discipline in our lives as He deals with specific sins and motives. We need to repent daily upon our knees as we wrestle with God in prayer.

But we can be confident that God's work will be finished in our lives and we will walk with the redeemed.